Ancestors — Guide To Discovery:

Key Principles and Processes of Family History Research

By Jim Tyrrell

Produced by KBYU Television in cooperation with Wisteria Pictures Inc.

KBYU gratefully acknowledges Ancestral Quest Inc. for their time and expertise as well as their many valuable resources used in publishing this companion book to the Ancestors series.

For more information on Ancestral Quest Inc., visit their website at www.ancestralquest.com.

Sunday morning breakfast

For information about this and other Ancestors products, visit the World Wide Web at
www.kbyu.org/ancestors

Library of Congress Cataloging-in-Publication Data

Tyrrell, Jim, 1946-
    Ancestors, guide to discovery: key principles and processes of family history research / Jim Tyrrell.
        p. cm.
    ISBN 1-890895-04-0
    1. Genealogy--Popular works. 2. United States--Genealogy--Popular works. I. Title.

CS16.T97 2000
929.1072--dc21

                                            00-036217

Cover design by Darrel B. Chamberlain with assistance from Jennifer E. Dahl and Michael Walker
Interior design by Darrel B. Chamberlain, Jonathan Brown and Elise Rasband,
with assistance from Susan Benhardt, Anna K. Brown and Jim Tyrrell
Original photography by Susan Benhardt.
Illustrations by Jonathan Brown
Credits and permissions for photographs on page ix.

Printed in the United States of America
10 9 8 7 6 5 4 3 2 1

Forward

Family—the international common denominator. It crosses all continents, races, languages, religions and time periods. Engage in conversation with anyone about any other subject and you may end up with differing opinions. But ask someone to tell you about their family and you will nurture a relationship that may last a lifetime. Each person who has ever lived contributes to the fabric of human existence. Their coming may be heard long before their birth as one hears and senses the coming of a distant train. Mothers, and sometimes fathers, sense each coming child. Once born, their lives resonate for whatever period of time they sojourn here on earth long after their death. In short, we are each touched in some way by their existence.

Somewhere during a child's maturing, the discovery process leads them to realize that they are part of something greater than themselves. Coupled with the natural curiosity of a child, they soon begin asking the obvious questions. "Where did I come from?" "Who were grandpa and grandma's parents?" With each answer, another question. Sometimes the unanswered questions linger well into adulthood. Sooner or later, the questions lead to areas unknown to the person responding. Ancestors Guide to Discovery is crafted to assist anyone desiring to find the answers to fill in the missing pieces of information in their family history. It is intended for those who have always wanted to know more about their families, but didn't know quite where to start.

As the companion to the Ancestors series, this publication builds upon the interest generated by viewing the weekly segments. With a common sense approach to discovering more about your family, it is founded on sound discovery principles and masterfully illustrated. Specific instructions on how, when, and where to proceed to discover the missing pieces of information make this a valuable resource for those whose interest has now propelled them to action.

With each new person that compiles information about their ancestry, generations of descendants benefit. Individually, our lives are worth noting, recording and folding into the history of each family. Together, we make up the history of communities, societies, and nations. Any effort to record some aspect of a person's life or family is worth whatever time or resources are needed. Seeing that they are preserved for future generations is vital to completing the effort. So as you gather share what you learn with other family members. Consider submitting copies of your efforts to your local genealogical society, historical society or one of the many family trees now found on the Internet. This may ensure that your family is remembered well into the future.

David E. Rencher
Director, Family History Library

ACKNOWLEDGEMENTS

KBYU Television gratefully acknowledges those who designed, contributed to and funded

Ancestors - Guide To Discovery:

Key Principles and Processes of Family History Research.

Author

Jim Tyrrell

Graphic Design and Layout

The landscapes of information and visual images for *Ancestors: Guide to Discovery* were created by
Darrel Chamberlain, Jonathan Brown and Elise Rasband, with assistance from
Susan Benhardt, Anna K. Brown and Jim Tyrrell.
Original photography by Susan Benhardt.
Illustrations by Jonathan Brown
Cover design by Darrel Chamberlain, with assistance from
Jennifer E. Dahl and Michael Walker.

Author Acknowledgments

Over the years of distilling the concepts highlighted in this book
several individuals have provided specific insights and encouragement. They include:
Don Jessee, Ruth Maness, Irene Johnson, Noel Cardon, Kay Merkley, Marcy Brown and Carol Clark.
In addition, many others along the way have contributed ideas, suggestions and assistance in producing this guide.
They include: Annette Tanner, Max Cropper, Roland Thatcher, Vern Reed, Randy Shoemaker, Kory Meyerink,
David Dilts, Nadine Timothy, Elaine Hasleton, Cindy Lee Banks, Jimmy B. Parker, Daris Williams,
Kim Woodbury, Megan Smolenyak, Mark Phillips, Melissa Puente,
Charlene Brown and Suzanne Erskine.

Perhaps the greatest contribution of all came from my own family.
To my wife Rita and our children, I thank you for all of the support, sacrifices and
schedule adjustments you have made, so that
I would have the time to work on and complete this project.

Funding

Major funding for the **Ancestors** project was provided by
Ancestral Quest
the George S. and Dolores Doré Eccles Foundation;
and Brigham Young University

with additional support from
U.S. Bank and the Brigham Young University Division of Continuing Education.

Research and content assistance was provided by the
Family History Department of The Church of Jesus Christ of Latter-day Saints,
Brigham Young University, and the Federation of Genealogical Societies.

The Ancestors Project

Ancestors - Guide to Discovery; Key Principles and Process of Family History Research is part of
Ancestors℠, an integrated media project
designed to teach the principles and processes of family history research.

In addition to this guide, the **Ancestors** project includes a series for public television, an interactive website, instructional video modules, a teacher's guide, a companion book and online enrichment courses.
For current information on the **Ancestors** project visit us online at
www.kbyu.org/ancestors.

Production

Ancestors was produced by KBYU Television in cooperation with Wisteria Pictures, Inc.
KBYU, a PBS member station located in Utah, is a service of Brigham Young University.
Wisteria Pictures is an independent media production company.

Photo by Susan Benhardt

ILLUSTRATIONS

CONTENT OVERVIEW

As you begin your journey of discovery about your ancestors, it is not important to know all of the information sources in the world. It is more important to clearly define the questions you want to answer about each ancestor. Then, you will better know which type of information sources to search for the answer to each question.

This guidebook will lead you through five steps to repeat over and over again to find the information you want. Each step outlines simple tasks to perform (see pages 2-29). Each task is explained and illustrated in the "how to" section (see pages 30-49). At the end of this guide is a Glossary and an Index to selected words and topics (see page 64). Also, you may duplicate the blank forms in the back for your personal use (see pages 71-79).

There is a growing mountain of information in the world that contains answers to questions.
Some of the information could be about your ancestors. Define your questions first.
Then you will know better which part of the mountain to search.

How To Complete The Steps

Forms

WELCOME TO A JOURNEY OF DISCOVERY

Most people at some time or other have wondered who their ancestors were, where they lived and what they did. The search for your ancestors — family history research — can change your life and bring many rewards.

In your journey, you will discover the names of your ancestors and the events of their lives. As you uncover the bits and pieces from memories, objects and records, you will begin to understand the conditions in which each of your ancestors lived. You will begin to feel connected to them.

From the information you find, you may be able to visualize their physical appearance. As you discover the details of each life event, you may begin to sense their character — the virtues and vices which governed their lives. You may feel indebted to them because of their examples of discipline, sacrifice, courage, love, and devotion to family and country. You might also discover traits and tendencies to avoid. In each case, you can learn the lessons of life. Your ancestors are a part of you! Your journey through the past is your opportunity to create and preserve a documented record of their lives.

BIRTH

IMMIGRATION

MARRIAGE

To learn about your ancestors has never been easier. Today's technology provides the tools to gather, organize and preserve information about your ancestors, and to share what you find with others.

People just like you have followed the five steps in this guidebook to uncover information. As you follow each step over and over again, you will find joy in the journey — a journey that can reunite you with your family from generations past and build a legacy for the future.

1. Write Down What You Know
2. Decide What You Want To Learn
3. Choose a Source of Information
4. Learn From The Source
5. Use What You Learned

MILITARY SERVICE

BOUGHT LAND

DEATH

SEPT. 16, 1934

The Journey Begins

Photo by Susan Benhardt

STEPS TO DISCOVER YOUR ANCESTORS

OVERVIEW

The five step process shown here will guide your search for information about the lives of your ancestors. Focus on information about one ancestor at a time. Follow the process over and over again to discover and verify information about each ancestor.

STEP **5** **Use What You Learn**
Evaluate the results of
your inquiry and share
your information with others.

STEP **4** **Learn From The Source**
Investigate the source for
the information you are
looking for.

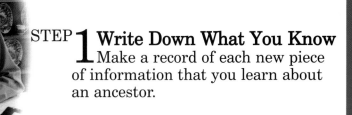

STEP **1** **Write Down What You Know**
Make a record of each new piece of information that you learn about an ancestor.

Write Down
What You Know

Decide What
You Want
To Learn

Choos
of Inf

STEP **2** **Decide What You Want To Learn**
Focus on one ancestor at a time. Then, choose and focus on one objective at a time about a life event or background topic.

STEP **3** **Choose a Source of Information**
Select a person, object or record that may contain the information you are looking for.

STEP 1: Write Down What You Know

Your parents, grandparents, great-grandparents, and all those generations beyond, are your ancestors. Information about their lives has been preserved in various ways. For example, you or other living relatives or family friends may have memories about them. Perhaps you know where written or printed records and documents are located about specific events in their lives. You might even know of some object that contains information about an event or relationship. As you begin your search, plan to write down each piece of information that you learn about. Also, plan to write down the name of the person, object or record where you got each piece of information. As you begin to piece together the information about your family from memories, documents and objects, you will begin to feel the joy and personal connection to your ancestors.

For each ancestor, use a Source Notes form write the name of the source and the informa collected.
(see page 73 for a blank form)

For each couple on the Pedigree Chart, write the names of the husband, wife and their children on the Family Group Record.
(see page 67 for a blank form)

Write four generations of information on the Pedigree Chart.
(see page 75 for a blank form)

Your parents (on lines 2 and 3)
Your grandparents (on lines 4-7)
Your great-grandparents (on lines 8-15)
You (on line 1)

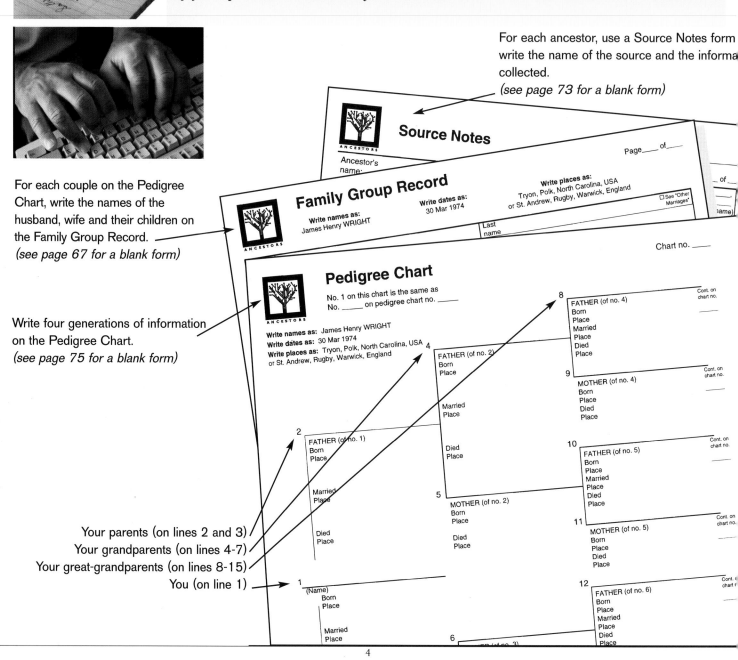

Recall Family Information

Contact Others With Family Memories

Find Documents, Writings, or Objects

Organize and Store Information

Your filing system should:
- Be simple
- Keep your records safe
- Help you find your information quickly

DO THIS

Write down what you have learned. Use a pencil and forms or a genealogy computer program to make a record of the information you have found.

1. Recall information about your ancestors, from your own memory, and write it down.

2. Ask family members and friends to recall information about your ancestors and write it down.
   Use a notebook and pencil, camera, audio tape recorder or video camera.

3. Gather individual and family documents, writings and objects.
   Separate out the relevant information and write it down.
   Make copies if you cannot take possession of the actual item.

4. Organize, in a way that is easy for you to use, the information you have gathered and written.

MORE INFORMATION

IN THIS BOOK:
- How to Prepare and Conduct an Oral History Interview, page 30
- How to Gather and Organize Family Information, page 32
- What to Look for in the Records You Find, page 34
- How to Fill Out a Pedigree Chart and Family Group Record, page 36
- How to Create Notes and Describe Information Sources, page 38
- Understand and Use the World of Information, page 42
- How to Evaluate Evidence, page 46

IN OTHER BOOKS:
- *Organizing Your Family History Search: Efficient & Effective Ways to Gather and Protect Your Genealogical Research,* by Sharon DeBartolo Carmack, (Cincinnati, Ohio: Betterway Books,1999)
- *The Everything Family Tree Book: Finding, Charting, and Preserving Your Family History,* by William G. Hartley, (Holbrook, Massachussetts: Adams Media Corp., 1998)
- *Unpuzzling Your Past: A Basic Guide to Genealogy,* by Emily Anne Croom (Cincinnati, Ohio: Betterway Books, 1995)
- *Record and Remember: Tracing Your Roots Through Oral History,* by Ellen Epstein and Jane Lewit (Scarborough House,)

ON THE WORLD WIDE WEB:
- *Ancestors* <www.kbyu.org/ancestors/>
- *Cyndi's List of Genealogy Sites on the Internet* <www.cyndislist.com/oral.htm>
- *Ancestry.com* <www.ancestry.com/learn/main.htm/>

STEP 2: Decide What You Want to Learn

This is probably the most important step in the process. This step will focus your search on one person and one question at a time. When you have clearly defined the question you want to learn the answer to, you will more clearly understand the best possible source of information to search for the answer. One question points you in one direction to search. Several questions point you in several directions to search. You can only go in one direction at a time, so keep your focus clear and simple! In time, as you follow this process, you can seek the answers to all of your questions.

Use these forms to identify missing and unverified information and clues about your ancestors.

Example:
Noah Williams* and his family.

Source Notes

Date: _____
Page _____

Ancestor's name: _Noah_ _____ _WILLIAMS_
First   Middle
Born: _____ Married: _____

☑ Male
☐ Female

This person is on pedigree chart nu line number _4_ , and/or is child nu on the family group record of (Husba

David WILLIAMS

☐ **Record**

Noah Williams

Date _____

/ Microfilm/fiche #

ults, analysis of

Family Group Record

Write names as:
James Henry WRIGHT

Write dates as:

Write places as:
Tryon, Polk, North Carolina, USA

Page _1_ of _2_

Husband _David_
Given name(s)
Born (day month year)
Died
Buried
Married
Husband's father
Given name(s)
Husband's mother
Given name(s)

Wife _Matilda_
Given name(s)
Born (day month year)
Died
Buried
Married
Wife's father
Given name(s)
Wife's mother
Given name(s)

Children List each child (whether li
1 Given name(s) _William_
Born (day month year)
Died
Buried
Spouse Given name(s)
Married

2 Given name(s) _Margaret_
Born (day month year)
Died
Buried
Spouse Given name(s)
Married

3 Given name(s) _Noah_
Born (day month year)
Died
Buried _1912?_
Spouse Given name(s)
Married

Other Marriages

Pedigree Chart

Chart no. _1_

No. 1 on this chart is the same as
No. _____ on pedigree chart no. _____

Write names as: James Henry WRIGHT
Write dates as: 30 Mar 1974
Write places as: Tryon, Polk, North Carolina, USA
or St. Andrew, Rugby, Warwick, England

8 _David WILLIAMS_
FATHER (of no. 4)
Born
Place _Kent, ?, England_
Married _Wales_
Place
Died
Place
Cont. on chart no. _____

4 _Noah WILLIAMS_
FATHER (of no. 2)
Born
Place _____ _Wales_
Married
Place _Logan, Cache, Utah_
Died _____ _1912_
Place _Chester, Fremont, Id_

9 _Matilda_
MOTHER (of no. 4)
Born
Place
Died
Place
Cont. on chart no. _____

?

2 _Gomer Hugh WILLIAMS_
FATHER (of no. 1)
Born _17 Feb 1900_
Place _Chester, Frmnt, Id_
Married _26 Jun 1931_
Place _Logan, Cache, Ut_
Died _7 Jan 1996_
Place _Chester, Fremont, Idaho_

5 _Elisa MUNK_
MOTHER (of no. 2)
Born _1866_
Place _Logan, Ut_
Died _22 Jun 1945_
Place _St. Anthony, Fremont, Id_

10 _Hans Jergens MUNK_
FATHER (of no. 5)
Born
Place _Denmark_
Married
Place
Died
Place
Cont. on chart no. _____

11 _Kristine Sorensen_
MOTHER (of no. 5)
Born
Cont. on chart no. _____

1 _Darris Eldon WILLIAMS_
(Name)
Born _24 Oct 1944_
Place _St. Anthony, Fremont, ID_
Married
Place
Died
Place

SPOUSE (of no. 1)

3 _Dorothy Elnora HOWARD_
MOTHER (of no. 1)
Born _11 Nov 1914_
Place _St. Anthony, Fremont, Idaho U.S.A._
Died _24 Oct 1944_
Place _St. Anthony, Fremont, Id_

6 _William HO_
FATHER (
Born
Place
Married
Place
Died
Place

7 _Rachel THOMPSON_
MOTHER (of no. 3)
Born
Place
Died
Place _1973_
Idaho Falls, Idaho, United States

Born
Place
Married
Place
Died
Place
Cont. on chart no. _____

15 _Rhoda DAVIS_
MOTHER (of no. 7)
Born
Place
Died
Place
Cont. on chart no. _____

When you choose a research objective,
if you are not familiar with the place where an event may have happened, consider the need to first learn about any or all of these:
• History and or geography of the place
• Culture (that includes the religions, social life and customs, ethnic groups and folklore) of the place.
• Language spoken.
• Record repositories (the places where records may be stored).
• Research guides (to learn how to conduct family history research) in that place.

Use these forms to focus your search on new information about one ancestor at a time.

For each ancestor, use a Research Log to focus on one ancestor and one research objective at a time.
(see page 71 for a blank form)

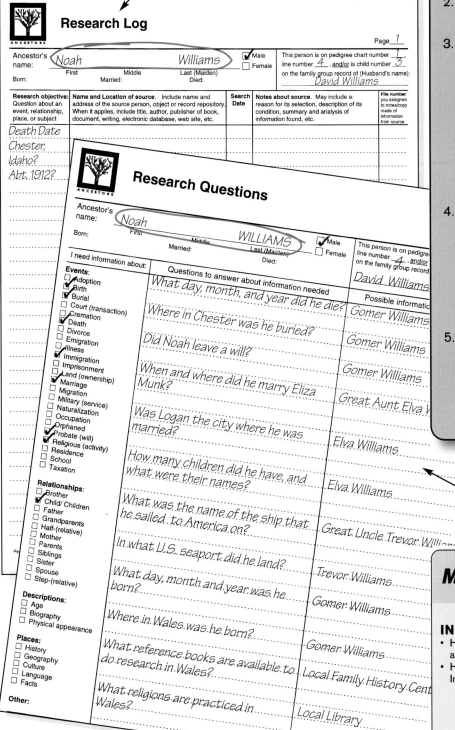

Research Log

Page 1

Ancestor's name: Noah Williams
First / Middle / Last (Maiden)
☑ Male ☐ Female

Born: Married: Died:

This person is on pedigree chart number ___, line number 4, and/or is child number 3 on the family group record of (Husband's name): David Williams

Research objective: Question about an event, relationship, place, or subject	Name and Location of source. Include name and address of the source person, object or record repository. When it applies, include title, author, publisher of book, document, writing, electronic database, web site, etc.	Search Date	Notes about source. May include a: reason for its selection, description of its condition, summary and analysis of information found, etc.	File number you assigned to notes/copy made of information from source
Death Date Chester, Idaho? Abt. 1912?				

Research Questions

Ancestor's name: Noah WILLIAMS
First / Middle / Last (Maiden)
☑ Male ☐ Female

Born: Married: Died:

This person is on pedigree line number 4, and/or on the family group record David Williams

I need information about:

Events:
☐ Adoption
☑ Birth
☑ Burial
☐ Court (transaction)
☑ Cremation
☑ Death
☐ Divorce
☐ Emigration
☐ Illness
☑ Immigration
☐ Imprisonment
☑ Land (ownership)
☑ Marriage
☐ Migration
☐ Military (service)
☐ Naturalization
☐ Occupation
☑ Orphaned
☑ Probate (will)
☑ Religious (activity)
☐ Residence
☐ School
☐ Taxation

Relationships:
☐ Brother
☑ Child/ Children
☐ Father
☐ Grandparents
☐ Half-(relative)
☐ Mother
☐ Parents
☐ Siblings
☐ Sister
☐ Spouse
☐ Step-(relative)

Descriptions:
☐ Age
☐ Biography
☐ Physical appearance

Places:
☐ History
☐ Geography
☐ Culture
☐ Language
☐ Facts

Other:

Questions to answer about information needed	Possible information
What day, month, and year did he die?	Gomer Williams
Where in Chester was he buried?	Gomer Williams
Did Noah leave a will?	Gomer Williams
When and where did he marry Eliza Munk?	Great Aunt Elva W.
Was Logan the city where he was married?	Elva Williams
How many children did he have, and what were their names?	Elva Williams
What was the name of the ship that he sailed to America on?	Great Uncle Trevor Williams
In what U.S. seaport did he land?	Trevor Williams
What day, month and year was he born?	Gomer Williams
Where in Wales was he born?	Gomer Williams
What reference books are available to do research in Wales?	Local Family History Cent
What religions are practiced in Wales?	Local Library

For each ancestor, use the Research Questions form to identify and list questions as possible research objectives.
(see page 69 for a blank form)

DO THIS

1. Look on your pedigree charts and family group records for direct line ancestors or other relatives who have missing or unverified information.

2. Choose one person to learn more about.

3. Form questions about the missing or unverified information for the person.

   Write questions about vital events, biographical events or background information. Verify and document presumed facts that have not been traced to:
   • A person who knows first hand or
   • An object or record that contains the information.

4. Choose one question at a time as your research objective.

   If you have questions about life events, seek to learn information about a later life event (such as death), before seeking to learn about an earlier life event (such as marriage or birth).

5. Write the ancestor's name and research objective on a Research Log. Use this Research Log to keep your research focused.

MORE INFORMATION

IN THIS BOOK:
• How to Write Research Questions and Fill Out a Research Log, page 40
• How to Create Source Note and Describe Information Sources, page 38

* Note: For the purpose of instruction, some information about Noah Williams and his family has been modified on these pages, and other pages that follow.

FIVE STEP PROCESS – STEP 2

STEP 3: Choose a Source of Information

There are three general sources of information that might have the answer to your research question. One source might be a relative or family friend with memories of the information. Another source might be an object with information inscribed, etched, sewn onto it, etc. Finally, a third source might be public and/or private records. Try to link yourself to your ancestors using evidence from reliable sources.

Choose a Person

Uncle Trevor

Great Aunt Elva

Grandpa Gomer

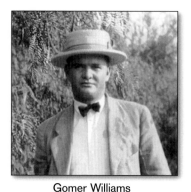

Gomer Williams

OR

Choose an Object

Noah Williams' Gravestone

Noah's watch given to Trevor
Death date inscribed inside

Noah Williams' Gravestone

OR

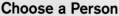

Choose a Record

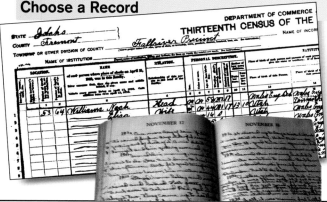

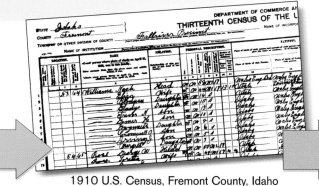

1910 U.S. Census, Fremont County, Idaho

FIVE STEP PROCESS – STEP 3

Research Log

Page____

Ancestor's name:	*Noah*	*WILLIAMS*	☑ Male	This person is on pedigree chart number _1_,
	First	Middle	Last (Maiden)	☐ Female	line number _4_ , and/or is child number _3_
Born:		Married:	Died:		on the family group record of (Husband's name):
					David Williams

Research objective: Question about an event, relationship, place, or subject	Name and Location of source. Include name and address of the source person, object or record repository. When it applies, include title, author, publisher of book, document, writing, electronic database, web site, etc.	Search Date	Notes about source. May include a: reason for its selection, description of its condition, summary and analysis of information found, etc.	File number you assigned to notes/copy made of information from source
Death Date?	*Gomer Williams, 923 Florence Ln., Chester, ID, USA;*			
Approx. 1912?	*interviewed by Daris Williams, 3 Apr 1990 at Chester,*			
Chester, Idaho?	*ID, USA; audio tape and notes in possession of Daris*			
	Williams, 374 Ventnor Ave., Denver, CO, USA			

If you select a person as your source, fill out your Research Log and turn to Step 4 on page 24.

Research Log

Page____

Ancestor's name:	*Noah*	*WILLIAMS*	☑ Male	This person is on pedigree chart number _1_,
	First	Middle	Last (Maiden)	☐ Female	line number _4_ , and/or is child number _3_
Born:		Married:	Died:		on the family group record of (Husband's name):
					David Williams

Research objective: Question about an event, relationship, place, or subject	Name and Location of source. Include name and address of the source person, object or record repository. When it applies, include title, author, publisher of book, document, writing, electronic database, web site, etc.	Search Date	Notes about source. May include a: reason for its selection, description of its condition, summary and analysis of information found, etc.	File number you assigned to notes/copy made of information from source
Death Date?	*Gravestone; Chester Cemetery, Chester, Fremont*			
Approx. 1912?	*County, ID, USA; (1.5 miles East of Chester on 800 N.*			
Chester, Idaho?	*Road); Notes and photograph made on 6 June 1990*			
	by Daris Williams; 374 Ventnor Ave., Denver, CO, USA			

If you select an object as your source, fill out your Research Log and turn Step 4 on page 24.

Research Log

Page____

Ancestor's name:	*Noah*	*WILLIAMS*	☑ Male	This person is on pedigree chart number _1_,
	First	Middle	Last (Maiden)	☐ Female	line number _4_ , and/or is child number _3_
Born:		Married:	Died:		on the family group record of (Husband's name):
					David Williams

Research objective: Question about an event, relationship, place, or subject	Name and Location of source. Include name and address of the source person, object or record repository. When it applies, include title, author, publisher of book, document, writing, electronic database, web site, etc.	Search Date	Notes about source. May include a: reason for its selection, description of its condition, summary and analysis of information found, etc.	File number you assigned to notes/copy made of information from source
Death Date?	*U.S. Bureau of Census, 1910 U.S. census, Fremont*			
Approx. 1912?	*County, Idaho; Fall River Precinct, Enumeration; Family*			
Chester, Idaho?	*History Library, Salt Lake City, UT*			
	microfilm # 1374237.			

If you select a record as your source, turn to page 10 to match your research objective with a record type.

DO THIS

1. Think about the possible sources that may have the information you are searching for and choose one.

2. Describe the source (person, object or record) on your Research Log.
   - If the source is a person, write his or her name, street address, city, state or province, country and phone number. Then, turn to Step 4 on page 24.
   - If the source is an object, write the name of the object and its location (street address, city, state or province and country). Then, turn to Step 4 on page 24.
   - If the source is a record, select a record to search. (See page 10.) Then, write the title, author and publisher of the record and its location (street address, city, state or province and country).

As you continue your research about this ancestor, you will have a complete record of the sources that you have already contacted or searched.

MORE INFORMATION

IN THIS BOOK:

- Understand and Use The World of Information, page 42

STEP 3: Choose a Source of Information (cont'd)

Select a type of record. Why select a type of record first? Most record repositories† have a catalog* of records. Each record in the catalog is described, grouped and listed under a specific record type. If you have a clear question as your research objective, the chart below will guide you to the type of record to look for.

If your research objective is to find information about . . .

If your research objective is to find information about . . .

If your research objective is to find information about . . .

LEGEND

† A record repository is any place where records are stored, such as a library, Family History Center, archive, courthouse, home, etc. Note: Family History Centers are branches of the Family History Library of The Church of Jesus Christ of Latter-day Saints in Salt Lake City, Utah, USA. More than 3500 centers are available to the public, throughout the world, at no charge.

* A catalog lists and describes each record (vital event, biographical and background information). For example, the Family History Library Catalog lists and describes each of the records in the Family History Library.

Match your research objective with a record type

A vital event in the life of a person, including:

- Birth
- Marriage
- Death

Then . . . → Go to Step 3A on page 12: Choose a Record Type That Contains Vital Event Information

A biographical event or personal description and relationship of a person, including:

- Adoption
- Burial
- Citizenship
- City or parish of foreign birth
- Country of foreign birth
- Debt
- Divorce
- Foreign place of origin
- Illness
- Imprisonment
- Living relatives
- Migration
- Military service
- Naming customs
- Occupation
- Orphaned
- Place where lived
- Property owned
- Public or legal transactions
- Religious activity
- School
- Servitude

Personal descriptions, characteristics and relationships

- Age
- Relatives (parents, children, spouse)
- Maiden name
- Physical description

Then . . . → Go to Step 3B on page 14: Choose a Record Type That Contains Biographical Information

Background information

- History (of places or groups)
- Geography (of places)
- Culture (related to religious, social and ethnic groups)
- Language (including the handwriting of a culture)
- Facts (about places or groups)
- Record Repositories (where records are kept)
- Instructions (related to conducting research in a specific place)

Then . . . → Go to Step 3C on page 18: Choose a Record Type That Contains Background Information

FIVE STEP PROCESS – STEP 3 (CONT'D)

STEP 3A: Choose a Record Type That Contains Vital Event Information

Vital event information includes the personal names, place names and dates about the events of birth, marriage and death.

Descriptions of compiled records and record types that contain vital event information are listed below

Ancestral File:
Over 35 million names organized into families and pedigrees. (See page 13.)

Bible Records:
Pages from family Bibles which record births, marriages, deaths, family relationships, and some genealogies. These pages may have been copied, collected, or indexed by family name.

Cemeteries:
Records about burial places, tombstone and monument inscriptions, records of sextons, lists of the buried, cemetery landscape and design, or how to copy gravestones or take rubbings. May give birth, marriage, and family information.

Census:
An official count of a people taken by government or church. Depending on the place and time, it may be sketchy (only the name of the head of household and the number of persons living there) or detailed (names of all people in household, ages, sex, occupation, income, etc.).

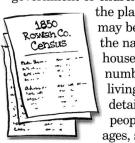

Church Records:
Records of Christian churches that often give information about christenings, baptisms, marriages, and deaths, as well as church membership and other things. In many places, churches kept the only official records.

Civil Registration:
Official records of vital information (births, marriages, and deaths) kept by civil leaders outside the United States and Canada.

Compiled Records:
Information that has been gathered from various sources and compiled as a record of events, relationships, circumstances, often in the form of biographies, family histories, etc.

Divorce Records:
Collections of records of divorces and annulments.

Family Histories:
Records that contain genealogical information, biographical sketches, or stories about members or branches of a family, or those having a common surname.

Funeral Homes:
Records that pertain to funeral homes or mortuaries and include business records, burial expenses, and information on the deceased.

International Genealogical Index:
Over 600 million names extracted from vital records from around the world. (See page 13.)

Land and Property:
Records (private and civil) about the ownership and transfer of land and other property that include deeds, mortgages, brands, and marks of ownership.

Military Records:
Military service records and lists of primarily men and boys who are serving, have served, or are eligible to serve in the armed forces. May include pensions, muster, or discharge lists.

Newspapers:
Copies, clippings, or complete newspapers which usually contain birth, marriage, and death announcements.

Obituaries:
Notices or lists of deaths, often with biographical sketches, usually from newspapers. May include funeral sermons.

Probate Records:
Records, wills, settlements, court proceedings, laws, etc., that deal with a person's estate at death. May include names of relatives.

Town Records:
Records of local civil governments, especially in New England and New York. May contain records of births, marriages, deaths, property, names of officials, tax rolls, business transactions, minutes, etc.

Vital Records:
Collections of records of births, marriages, or deaths. In the United States, these include official government records.

DO THIS

IF your research objective is to find information about Birth · Marriage · Death

FIRST, look for your ancestor's name in compiled records, such as the following located in a Family History Center † . . .

- ANCESTRAL FILE (available in the FamilySearch™ computer program, or on the World Wide Web*).

OR

- The INTERNATIONAL GENEALOGICAL INDEX (IGI) (available on microfiche and in the FamilySearch computer program, or on the World Wide Web*).

OR

- FAMILY HISTORIES. Look for your ancestor's surname in the Family History Library Catalog° Surname section, (available on microfiche and in the FamilySearch computer program, or on the World Wide Web*).

THEN, if you do not find information in the compiled records, such as the ones above, look for one of the record types listed under your research objective below . . .

Birth
- Vital records or Civil Registration
- Church records
- Census
- Emigration and Immigration
- Naturalization and citizenship
- Bible records
- Cemeteries
- Obituaries
- Military Records
- Town records
- Newspapers
- Occupations

Marriage
- Vital records or Civil Registration
- Church records
- Newspapers
- Bible records
- Military Records
- Divorce records
- Land and Property
- Town records

Death
- Vital records or Civil Registration
- Cemeteries
- Probate records
- Church records
- Obituaries
- Bible records
- Military Records
- Funeral homes
- Town records

Note: If you searched all available record types in a record repository and have not found a record, contact another repository where the type of record you are looking for may be stored.

LEGEND

† Family History Centers are branches of the Family History Library. This library is the largest genealogical library of its kind in the world. It is owned and operated by The Church of Jesus Christ of Latter-day Saints in Salt Lake City, Utah, USA. More than 3500 centers are available to the public, throughout the world, at no charge.

° A catalog lists and describes each record, in a record repository's collection. For example, the Family History Library Catalog lists and describes the records in the Family History Library. Similar catalogs exist for most libraries and archives around the world.

* The address for the FamilySearch program on the World Wide Web is www.familysearch.org.

Go to page 20 to choose a possible repository where this type of record is stored.

STEP 3B: Choose a Record Type That Contains Biographical Information

Biographical information includes non vital events (for example, information about work, immigration, military service, schools attended, places where an ancestor lived, etc.). It also may include personal descriptions, characteristics and relationships.

Descriptions of record types that contain biographical information are listed below and continued on page 16.

continued on page 16.

Bible Records:
Pages from family Bibles which record births, marriages, deaths, family relationships, and some genealogies. These pages may have been copied, collected, or indexed by family name.

Biography:
A brief or full history of the life of a person. May include birth, marriage, death, family information, places lived, and major events. Prominent people are most likely to be listed.

Buddhist Records:
Records, documents, or registers created by Buddhist sects which usually include information on deaths.

Business Records and Commerce:
Account books, ledgers, or papers about a business or company. May contain company histories and lists of officers and employees.

Cemeteries:
Records about burial places, tombstone and monument inscriptions, records of sextons and lists of the buried. May contain information about cemetery landscape and design, or how to copy gravestones or take rubbings. May give birth, marriage, and family information.

Census:
An official count of a people taken by government or church. Depending on the place and time, it may be sketchy (only the name of the head of household and the number of persons living there) or detailed (names of all people in household, ages, sex, occupation, income, etc.).

Church Records:
Records of Christian churches, often giving information about christenings or baptisms, marriages, and deaths, as well as church membership and other things. In many places, churches kept the only official records.

Civil Registration:
Official records of vital information (births, marriages, and deaths) kept by civil leaders outside the United States and Canada.

DO THIS

FIRST, find your research objective in the columns below. THEN, choose one of the record types next to it.

Adoption	Guardianship, Genealogy, Census, Biography, Court Records, Probate Records, Church Records, Directories, Obituaries, Societies
Age	Vital Records or Civil Registration, Census, Cemeteries, Military Records
Burial	Cemeteries, Obituaries, Vital records or Civil Registration, Church Records, Funeral Homes, Town Records
Citizenship	Naturalization and Citizenship, Biography
City or parish of foreign birth	Church Records, Naturalization and Citizenship, Genealogy, Biography, Vital Records, Civil Registration, Newspapers, History, Emigration and Immigration
Country of foreign birth	Church Records, Civil Registration, Naturalization and Citizenship, Census Records, Emigration and Immigration
Debt	Poorhouses, Poor Law
Divorce	Divorce Records, Court Records, Vital Records or Civil Registration, Newspapers
Foreign place of origin	Emigration and Immigration, Census, Naturalization and Citizenship, Church Records, Military Records
Illness	Medical Records
Imprisonment	Correctional Institutions, Concentration Camps
Living relatives	Genealogy, Directories, Court Records, Obituaries, Census, Biography, Societies, Church Records, Probate Records
Maiden name	Vital Records or Civil Registration, Cemeteries, Probate Records, Church Records, Bible Records, Obituaries, Newspapers, Military Records

Migration	Emigration and Immigration, Census, Naturalization and Citizenship, Genealogy, Biography, Newspapers
Military service	Military Records
Naming customs	Names-Personal, Social Life and Customs
Occupation	Census, Directories (city), Pensions, Emigration and Immigration, Officials and Employees, Court Records, Business Records and Commerce, Newspapers, Merchant Marine
(being) Orphaned	Orphans and Orphanages, Guardianship
Physical description	Vital Records or Civil Registration, Naturalization and Citizenship, Emigration and Immigration, Biography, Military Records, Genealogy, Personal Journals
Place where lived	Census, Directories (city), Land and Property, Taxation, Voting Registers, Church Records, History, Military Records
Property owned	Probate Records, Land and Property, Taxation, Manors
Public or legal transactions	Court Records, Public Records, Newspapers, Notarial Records
Relatives (parents, children, spouse)	Vital Records or Civil Registration, Church Records, Bible Records, Census, Probate Records, Emigration and Immigration, Obituaries, Notarial Records, Naturalization and Citizenship
Religious activity	Church Records, Jewish Records, Buddhist Records, Hindu Records, Islamic Records, Shinto Records, History, Biography, Census, Cemeteries
School	Schools
Servitude	Slavery and Bondage

NOTE: If you have searched all available record types in a record repository and have not found a record, contact another repository where the type of record may be stored.

Go to page 20 to choose a possible repository where this type of record may be stored.

STEP 3B: Choose a Record Type That Contains Biographical Information (cont'd)

Descriptions of record types that contain biographical information are continued below

Concentration Camps:
A written descriptive work pertaining to institutions who detain groups of people based on their race, religion, national origin, etc.

Correctional Institutions:
Records of institutions which confined people (those who committed crimes, debtors, etc.) as inmates. May list names of persons held there and their guardians.

Court Records:
Proceedings, actions, and discussions of various courts. Court records cover criminal offenses, licensing, contracts, divorce, probate, land and property, etc.

Directories:
Alphabetical or classified lists that include the names and addresses of (1) the inhabitants or organizations of a place, or (2) members of an organization.

Divorce Records:
Collections of records of divorces and annulments.

Emigration and Immigration:
Records about people moving out of or into a country. May contain lists of ship's passengers, people who bought tickets from a ticket agent, police registration on leaving or arriving in a country, etc. Does not include records of moves within a country.

Funeral Homes:
Records pertaining to funeral homes or mortuaries, including business records, burial expenses, and information on the deceased.

Genealogy:
Records that trace family ancestors or descendants, and family histories of many families who do not share a single surname. May have descriptions or charts of pedigrees, family trees, and family groups.

Guardianship:
Court decisions, legal records, and any information about a guardian's responsibility for a child, including adoption.

Hindu Records:
Records, documents, or registers created by Hindu sects which often contain birth, marriage, or death information.

Islamic Records:
Records, documents, or registers created by Islamic sects which often contain information on births, marriages, or deaths.

Jewish Records:
Records, documents, or registers of Jewish religious groups, usually giving information on births, marriages, or deaths.

Land and Property:
Records (private and civil) about the ownership and transfer of land and other property, including deeds, mortgages, brands, and marks of ownership.

Manors:
Records about the feudal manor system: descriptions of the lord, his lands, buildings, and dealings with people on the land. May include lists of people, genealogies, histories, and probate and civil court records. A manor was an English or Middle Ages estate under the ownership of a lord who had rights over land and tenants. This included the right to hold court.

Medical Records:
Records about the medical field: hospital records; records of doctors, midwives (babies delivered), or other practitioners; lists of patients; licenses; etc.

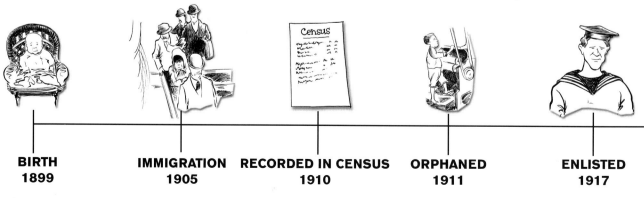

BIRTH	IMMIGRATION	RECORDED IN CENSUS	ORPHANED	ENLISTED
1899	1905	1910	1911	1917

Merchant Marine:
Works and records dealing with publicly- or privately-owned ships and their personnel.

Military Records:
Military service records and lists of primarily men and boys who are serving, have served, or are eligible to serve in the armed forces. May include pensions, muster, or discharge lists.

Naturalization and Citizenship:
Books, records, and laws concerning citizenship, the qualifications for, the process of, and country records. Includes oaths of allegiance and naturalization papers. May give birth, marriage, and family information.

Newspapers:
Copies, clippings, or complete newspapers which usually contain birth, marriage, and death announcements.

Notarial Records:
Records of notaries, who (in many places) verified business transactions, wills, marriage contracts, intention to marry, sale of land, etc.

Obituaries:
Notices or lists of deaths, often with biographical sketches, usually from newspapers. May include funeral sermons.

Officials and Employees:
Lists and records of government officials and employees, including international agencies and institutions under government direction.

Orphans or Orphanages:
Records about children raised or cared for by someone other than their parents (includes child-welfare cases). Name and age of child is usually given. May include descriptions of the institutions where these children lived.

Pensions:
Records of compensation for military service, employment, disability, reparation, etc. Includes lists of eligibility, names of family, wife or widow, heirs, etc.

Poorhouses, Poor Law, etc.:
Records about institutions that care for the poor, including lists of inmates, removal and settlement papers, and laws on care of the poor, etc.

Probate Records:
Records, wills, settlements, court proceedings, laws, etc., that deal with a person's estate at death. May include names of relatives.

Public Records:
Any records created by civil authorities which do not fit under other specific subject headings.

Schools:
Records about educational institutions. May contain lists of teachers, students, or graduates.

Shinto Records:
Records, documents, registers, etc., created by Shinto sects.

Slavery and Bondage:
Records about slaves, indentured servants, serfs, or those who have been freed. May have lists of people, deeds of people considered as property, etc.

Taxation:
Description of records of a tax system, including tax lists, lists of property, etc.

Town Records:
Records of local civil governments, especially in New England and New York. May contain records of births, marriages, deaths, property, names of officials, tax rolls, business transactions, minutes, etc.

Vital Records:
Collections of records of births, marriages, or deaths. In the United States, these include official government records.

Voting Registers:
Lists of registered or eligible voters of countries, cities, or electoral districts. May include heads of households only.

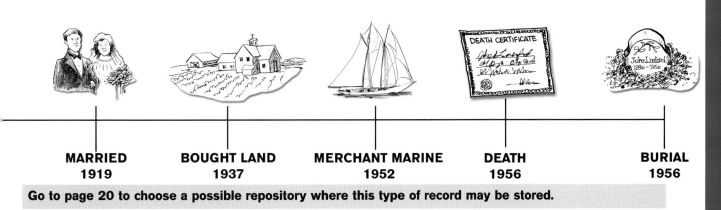

MARRIED	BOUGHT LAND	MERCHANT MARINE	DEATH	BURIAL
1919	1937	1952	1956	1956

Go to page 20 to choose a possible repository where this type of record may be stored.

STEP 3C: Choose a Record Type That Contains Background Information

Background information includes various sources that describe the setting, culture, language, etc., and can be used to understand the circumstances in which original documents and compiled records were created.

Descriptions of record types that contain background information are listed below

Almanacs:
Books that describe the events of one year (weather, floods, cycle of moon, statistics on people, etc.) for a place. They may give addresses of governments, organizations, or churches.

Archives and Libraries:
Descriptions of archives, libraries, museums, and other places where records are stored.

Centennial Celebrations, etc.:
Records of celebrations of historic events, anniversaries (100th, 50th, etc.) in which the history of a country, church, place, or organization may be told.

Chronology:
Records which tell how different people measure days, months, years, and keep track of time.

Church History:
Histories of Christian churches, which may be general (e.g., history of a denomination, worldwide) or specific (e.g., a certain church building, a Catholic parish, a Latter-day Saint ward, etc.).

Colonization:
Records of colonies in new lands, often with lists of persons, ethnic groups, and classes of people. Colonists may have been prisoners sent to settle new lands, free men enticed to go to new lands, those who chose to go to new lands, or those forced to leave their homelands.

Description and Travel:
Records about the geography of a place, which may include personal impressions and descriptions. Provide background material, historical descriptions, and social history.

Dictionaries:
Books of words and their definitions, arranged alphabetically. Dictionaries may define words used in one language or may contain words translated from one language to another.

Directories:
Alphabetical or classified lists that include the names and addresses of (1) the inhabitants or organizations of a place, or (2) members of an organization.

Dwellings:
Records about buildings and homes: the design, construction, traditions, etc. May discuss architecture generally (e.g., Georgian home styles) or note specifics (e.g., the buildings on one Scandinavian farm). Useful for background information for personal or family histories.

Encyclopedias and Dictionaries:
Records which inform concisely about many general subjects or which explain one subject thoroughly.

Ethnology:
Records about races of peoples: their traditions, origin, background; where or how they lived; their physical, social, and religious characteristics, etc.

Folklore:
Records of stories, tales, and oral traditions of a people. May discuss religious beliefs, explanations of creation of the world, and sagas that depict history and heroes.

Gazetteers:
Records which list geographical names alphabetically, often giving descriptions of those localities or their map coordinates.

Handbooks, Manuals, etc.:
Reference works in which facts and information pertaining to a certain subject are arranged for ready reference and consultation.

Handwriting:
Records about early forms of handwriting (alphabets, writing samples, instructions on how to decipher, etc.).

Heraldry:
Records about coats of arms, family crests, flags, emblems, seals, etc., and how they were devised, granted, or used.

Historical Geography:
Records about changes in boundaries, jurisdictions (civil or church), or territories at different times in history. May include background of prominent families, including genealogies.

History:
Descriptions of the past events of a place, an institution, or a field of knowledge.

Language and Languages:
Records that define, teach, or describe major languages and specific dialects.

Law and Legislation:
Records, histories, and descriptions of laws, codes, ordinances, etc.

Maps:
Maps, charts, or plans which may show current or historic locations of towns, buildings, boundaries, roads, rivers, railroads, parish boundaries, etc. Includes atlases.

Migration, Internal:
Records about the movement of people within a country. May show growth of cities, movement of tribes or ethnic groups, or population changes due to industrialization, famine, plague, etc.

Military History:
History of battles, wars, and armed forces (rarely includes names of soldiers).

Minorities:
Histories and descriptions of racial, ethnic, religious, or other groups of people who were a small segment, distinct from the larger population of an area.

Names, Geographical:
Books about names of places (geographical areas, countries, cities, street names, etc.), May give their origin, history, changes, or variations.

Names, Personal:
Books about names of persons, families, deities, businesses, or ethnic groups. May give variations, histories, meanings, origins, or uses.

Native Races:
Histories or descriptions of original peoples who lived in regions settled in modern times. Includes peoples such as American Indians, Australian Aborigines, Maori, etc.

Occupations:
Records that give general descriptions of a specific job or trade. Includes information on guilds, unions, apprenticeships, etc.

Periodicals:
Regularly issued magazines or journals containing various articles.

DO THIS

FIRST, find your research objective below.
THEN, choose one of the record types next to it.

History (of places or groups)	History, Colonization, Church History, Minorities, Periodicals, Chronology, Encyclopedias and Dictionaries, Centennial Celebrations, Migration-Internal, Law and Legislation, Military History, Yearbooks
Geography (of places)	Gazetteers, Maps, Historical Geography, Postal and Shipping Guides, Description and Travel, Names-Geographical
Culture (related to religious, social and ethnic groups)	Religion and Religious Life, Social Life and Customs, Minorities, Native Races, Ethnology, Folklore
Language (and hand-writing of a culture)	Language and Languages, Dictionaries, Handwriting
Facts (about places or groups)	Almanacs, Statistics, Politics and Government, Population, Occupations, Heraldry, Names-Personal, Dwellings
Record repositories (in a country, state, city, etc.)	Archives and Libraries, Directories, Societies
Instructions (related to conducting research in a specific place)	Handbooks, Manuals, etc., Periodicals

NOTE: If you have searched all available record types in a record repository and have not found any information, contact another record repository where the type of record may be stored.

Politics and Government:
Records about the politics or government of an area. This includes parliament discussions, feudal society, economic policy, national or local governments, etc.

Population:
Studies of population statistics of certain places which give such things as size and density, growth, migration, vital statistics, average family, historical changes, etc.

Postal and Shipping Guides:
List of post offices, railroad stations and stops, ports, terminals, etc., with place names and route information.

Religion and Religious Life:
Records about beliefs, customs, and practices of religious groups (rituals, tenets, etc.).

Social Life and Customs:
Records about manners, customs, ceremonies, traditions, and lifestyles of a certain place.

Societies:
Records of organizations, institutions, or groups active in particular field of interest. May include lists of members.

Statistics:
Numerical information about a place or topic, such as tallies, trends, census, population, etc.

Yearbooks:
Books that summarize the events of one year for a specific place, organization, or topic (such as demographics, farm production, government).

Go to page 20 to choose a possible repository where this type of record may be stored.

STEP 3D: Choose a Place Where Records Are Stored

People around the world have been creating and preserving records for thousands of years. Some people and places store only the records created by them. Other places have copies of records that were created in different parts of the world.

Match a record type with a place where records are stored

RECORD TYPE	PLACES WHERE RECORD TYPE MAY LIKELY BE STORED
Almanac	Local library or genealogical society
Archives and Libraries (lists of)	Local library near you
Bible Records	Home of family member; local genealogical society
Bibliography	Local library near you
Biography	Home of author; library; archive
Buddhist History	Genealogical society; library
Buddhist Records	Genealogical society; library
Business Records and Commerce	Company where records were created
Cemeteries	Cemetery office; local genealogical society
Census	National, provincial and state archive or library; local genealogical society
Centennial Celebrations etc.	Library; local genealogical society
Chronology	Library; local genealogical society
Church Directories	Library; archive; local genealogical society
Church History	Library; archive; local genealogical society
Church Records	Church's local archive; library; local genealogical society
Civil Registration	Government archive
Collected Works	Library; archive; local genealogical society
Collections	Library; archive; local genealogical society
Colonization	Library; archive; local genealogical society
Concentration Camps	Library; archive; local genealogical society
Correctional Institutions	Library; archive; local genealogical society
Court Records	Archive
Description and Travel	Library; local genealogical society

RECORD TYPE	PLACES WHERE RECORD TYPE MAY LIKELY BE STORED
Dictionaries	Library; archive
Directories	Library; archive
Divorce Records	Archive; courthouse
Dwellings	Library; archive; local genealogical society
Emigration and Immigration	Library; archive; local genealogical society
Encyclopedias and Dictionaries	Library
Ethnology	Library
Family Histories	Home of author; library; local genealogical society
Folklore	Library; local genealogical society
Funeral Homes	Library; archive; local genealogical society
Gazetteers	Library; local genealogical society
Genealogy	Library; local genealogical society
Guardianship	Library; archive
Guide Books	Library; archive; local genealogical society
Handbooks, Manuals, etc.	Library; archive; local genealogical society
Handwriting	Library
Heraldry	Library; archive; local genealogical society
Hindu History	Library; archive; local genealogical society
Hindu Records	Church archive
Historical Geography	Library; archive; local genealogical society
History	Library; archive; local genealogical society
Indexes	Library
Inventories, Registers, Catalogs	Library; archive; local genealogical society
Islamic History	Library; archive; local genealogical society
Islamic Records	Religion's local archive

Find original records stored close to the place where they were created.

Civil Governments of nations, states, provinces, counties, districts, cities and towns usually store their records in archives, libraries and courthouses.

Religious Organizations usually store their records in or near the facility where they were created. Records may also be stored in a local, regional or national archive or library for that religion.

Others - such as businesses, public institutions, hospitals, newspapers, funeral homes, cemeteries, schools, etc., usually store their records in or near the facility where they were created. Also, some records may have been given to a local historical society.

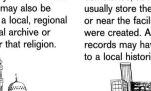

Find many records in the Family History Library or in a Family History Center near you.

The Family History Library in Salt Lake City, Utah, U.S.A. This library has the world's largest collection of genealogical information. The library is owned and operated by The Church of Jesus Christ of Latter-day Saints and is free to the public.

Family History Centers (Over 3,500 throughout the world.) The microfilmed records in the Family History Library in Salt Lake City, can be accessed through a Family History Center. Family History Centers are primarily located in LDS Church meetinghouses, and are open to the public.

RECORD TYPE	PLACES WHERE RECORD TYPE MAY LIKELY BE STORED
Jewish History	Library; archive; local genealogical society
Jewish Records	Religion's local archive
Land and Property	Library; archive; local genealogical society
Language and Languages	Library
Law and Legislation	Library
Manors	Library; archive; local genealogical society
Maps	Library; archive; local genealogical society
Medical Records	Library; archive; medical facility
Merchant Marine	Library; archive
Migration, Internal	Library; archive; local genealogical society
Military History	Library; archive; local genealogical society
Military Records	Library; archive; local genealogical society
Minorities	Library; archive; local genealogical society
Names, Geographical	Library; archive; local genealogical society
Names, Personal	Library
Native Races	Library; archive; local genealogical society
Naturalization and Citizenship	Library; archive
Newspapers	Library; newspaper archive; local genealogical society
Nobility	Library
Notarial Records	Library; archive; local genealogical society
Obituaries	Library; newspaper archive; local genealogical society
Occupations	Library; archive; local genealogical society
Officials and Employees	Library; archive; local genealogical society
Orphans or Orphanages	Library; archive; local genealogical society
Pensions	Library; archive; local genealogical society
Periodicals	Library; archive; local genealogical society
Politics and Government	Library; archive; local genealogical society
Poorhouses, Poor Law, etc.	Library; archive; local genealogical society
Population	Library; archive; local genealogical society
Portraits	Family members; library; archive; local genealogical society
Postal and Shipping Guides	Library; local genealogical society
Probate Records	Library; archive
Public Records	Library; archive; local genealogical society
Religion and Religious Life	Library; archive; local genealogical society

RECORD TYPE	PLACES WHERE RECORD TYPE MAY LIKELY BE STORED
Schools	Library; archive; local genealogical society
Shinto History	Library; archive
Shinto Records	Religion's local archive
Slavery and Bondage	Library; archive; local genealogical society
Social Life and Customs	Library; local genealogical society
Societies	Library; archive; local genealogical society
Sources	Library; local genealogical society
Statistics	Library
Taxation	Library; local genealogical society
Town Records	Library; archive; local genealogical society
Visitations, Heraldic	Library; archive; local genealogical society
Vital Records	Library; archive
Voting Registers	Library; archive; local genealogical society
Yearbooks	Library; local genealogical society

DO THIS

FIRST, find the type of record you are looking for on the chart.

THEN, select a place where you believe that record type may likely be stored.

NEXT, Contact a repository near you or near the areas where your ancestors lived.

Before you visit the archive, library, courthouse, society, or Family History Center, find out about the collection, hours open, services available, and fees.

MORE INFORMATION

In This Book:
- Places where records are stored, page 50
- How to Plan for a Research Trip or Hire a Professional Researcher, page 48
- How the Internet Works and Where to Search, page 44

In Other Books:
- Elizabeth Petty Bentley, *The Genealogist's Address Book*, 4th edition (Baltimore, Maryland: Genealogical Publishing Co., 1998)
- Juliana Szucs Smith, compiler, *The Ancestry Family Historian's Address Book : A Comprehensive List of Addresses of Local, State, & Federal Agencies & Institutions* (Orem, Utah: Ancestry, Inc., 1998)
- Jeane Eddy Westin, *Finding Your Roots: How to Trace Your Ancestors at Home and Abroad* (New York: Jeremy P. Tarcher/Putnam, 1998)

On The World Wide Web:
- Cyndi's List of Genealogical Sites on the Internet, Topical Category Index (Records), online <www.cyndislist.com/topical.htm#Records>

Find a stored copy of a record anywhere.

If one or more copies of a record was made, there is a good chance you can find it in one of the following places.

Local, State and National Historical and Genealogical Societies can be found around the world. These organizations collect valuable records about the local area.

Many city, county, college, university and private libraries throughout the world contain major collections of genealogical records. They often have copies of federal records, local and family histories, special collections for ethnic and religious groups, newspaper collections, etc.

The world's largest computer network is the Internet. It contains the World Wide Web, where genealogical information and records can be found.

STEP 3E: Choose a Specific Record to Search

Imagine for a minute that the type of record you wanted to find was in a big pile at the place where records are stored. The pile could contain books, maps, microfiche, microfilm and records on computer. To find a record in the pile would be frustrating and nearly impossible. Fortunately, a person called a cataloger was given the task to describe, number and categorize each item in the pile. All of the cataloger's descriptions together make up what is called the catalog.

Use the catalog of information sources in each library, archive, genealogical and historical society

A repository's collection may contain hundreds, thousands or even millions of cataloged items that include:

Original Records

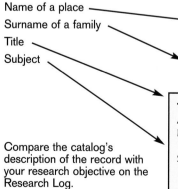

Original records contain facts that are recorded about an event at or near the time the event took place.

Compiled Records

Compiled records contain information that has been collected from various sources about a person, family or topic.

Background Information

Background information sources contain descriptions of the circumstances of life in a specific place during a given time period.

Finding Aids

Finding aids contain reference sources to find records.

Each item that is described in the catalog is called an entry. An entry can be a few lines long or thousands of lines long →

Surname:	**O'Neill**
Title:	Douglas, O'Neill, Touchstone families
Authors:	Hanson, Junia Douglas (Main Author)
Notes:	Microfilm of original typescript (26 leaves) in the Clayton Library, Houston, Texas.
	--
Subjects:	Douglas, O'Neill, Touchstone
Call Number:	1318398 Item 9 Location: FHL US/CAN Film
Format:	Manuscript (On Film) Language: English
Publication:	Salt Lake City : Filmed by the Genealogical Society of Utah, 1983
Physical:	on 1 microfilm reel : geneal. tables ; 35 mm.

Example of entry information in the Family History Library Catalog in Salt Lake City, Utah, U.S.A., and in over 3,500 Family History Centers around the world.

Use the catalog to search for the specific record you need.

The records in the repository's collection may be listed in the catalog under the:

Record Type

Name of a place
Surname of a family
Title
Subject

New York, Monroe, Rochester - Vital records

Title: Monroe County, New York marriage records of Rev. George Washington, 1846-1879 : founding minister of the First Universalist Society of the city of Rochester, he served as

Surname: Tyrrell

Title: Further genealogical notes on the Tyrrell-Terrell family of Virginia and its English and Norman French progenitors

Title:	**Huronia : a history and geography of the Huron Indians, 1600-1650**
Authors:	Heidenreich, Conrad, 1936-.
Notes:	Originally presented as the author's thesis, McMaster University.

Subjects:	Ontario - Native races
	Huron Indians
	Indians of North America - Ontario
Call Number:	970.3 H94lh Location: FHL US/CAN Book
Format:	Books/Monographs Language: English
Publication:	[Toronto] : McClelland and Stewart, c1971
ISBN/ISSN:	0770140768

Compare the catalog's description of the record with your research objective on the Research Log.

Remember, as you choose a record:

1. The catalog does not do research for you, decide what records to search for, or give detailed information about your ancestors.
2. If you have a choice between a record with an index and one without, choose the record with the index.
3. There may be skills and knowledge that you will need, so that you can choose or read some records.

Ability to read foreign language

Records are usually in the language of the country where they were created. You may need to use a dictionary of the language of the record, or find someone who can read the record for you.

Ability to read handwriting

In order to read many of the early records used in family history research, you will need to become familiar with the styles of writing used by those who wrote the records. The study of these styles is called paleography.

Knowledge of boundary changes

Some city, county, state and even country boundaries have changed over time. The place where a record was created and stored may now be part of a different jurisdiction. Consider possible boundary changes when you choose a record.

Knowledge of spelling variations

Standard spelling has not always been a concern in the creation of records. How a name was pronounced caused a listener to write the same name in various ways. Consider possible spelling variations of personal and place names. For example, the name Tyrrell could be spelled:

Tyril Tirel Tyrrall

Terel Tiril Tarrell

Taril Teral Turel

Knowledge of calendar changes

Be aware that Pope Gregory XIII revised the calendar in October, 1582. The French (1793-1806) and others have also revised the calendar.

Write a record description on the Research Log

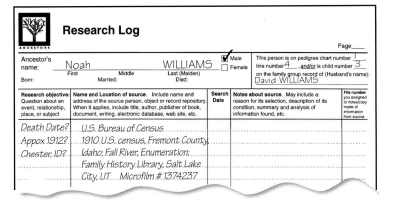

Research Log					Page____
Ancestor's name: Noah	WILLIAMS	☑ Male ☐ Female		This person is on pedigree chart number 1 line number 4, and/or is child number 3 on the family group record of (Husband's name): David WILLIAMS	
First Middle Last (Maiden)					
Born: Married: Died:					

Research objective: Question about an event, relationship, place, or subject	Name and Location of source. Include name and address of the source person, object or record repository. When it applies, include title, author, publisher of book, document, writing, electronic database, web site, etc.	Search Date	Notes about source. May include a: reason for its selection, description of its condition, summary and analysis of information found, etc.	File number you assigned to notes/copy made of information from source
Death Date? Appox 1912? Chester, ID?	U.S. Bureau of Census 1910 U.S. census, Fremont County, Idaho; Fall River, Enumeration; Family History Library, Salt Lake City, UT. Microfilm # 1374237			

The catalog entries are usually stored on a computer. However, some record repositories may have the entries stored on index cards in a file cabinet or on microfiche. The information described in the catalog is preserved in the form of books, periodicals, microfilms, microfiche, maps, and computer files.

MORE INFORMATION

In this Book
- How the Internet Works and Where to Search, page 44
- How to . . . Fill Out a Research Log, page 40

Books
- Emily Anne Croom, *Unpuzzling Your Past: A Basic Guide to Genealogy* (Cincinnati, Ohio: Betterway Books, 1995)
- Sandra H. Luebking (Editor), Loretto D. Szucs, *The Source: A Guidebook of American Genealogy*, Revised edition (Orem, Utah: Ancestry, Inc.,1997)
- Kathleen W. Hinckley, *Locating Lost Family Members & Friends: Modern Genealogical Research Techniques for Locating the People of Your Past and Present* (Cincinnati, Ohio: Betterway Books, 1999)
- Cyndi Howells, *Netting Your Ancestors Genealogical Research on the Internet* (Baltimore, Maryland: Genealogical Publishing Co., 1997)

World Wide Web Sites
- Cyndi's List of Genealogical Sites on the Internet, <www.cyndislist.com>
- FamilySearch Internet Genealogy Service <www.familysearch.org/Browse/browse.asp>

STEP 4: Learn From the Source

This step will bring you in direct contact with the source that might have the information you are looking for. Remember! Your research objective is the main reason that you chose the source of information. Listen for or look for information that will answer your research objective.

Meet with the Person

Gomer Williams

OR ## Locate the Object

Noah Williams' Gravestone

For a person, object, or record, make notes, take a photo, or make a video or audio recording of the source of the information.

OR ## Find the Record

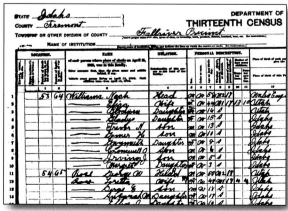

1910 U.S. Census, Fremont County, Idaho

Source

Ancestor's name: _Noah_

Research Log

Ancestor's name: _Noah_ _WILLIAMS_

Born: First   Middle   Last (Maiden)

Married:

Died:

Research objective: Question about an event, relationship, place, or subject	Name and Location of source. Include name and address of the source person, object or record repository. When it applies, include title, author, publisher of book, document, writing, electronic database, web site, etc.	Search Date
Death Date 1910 Census Appox 1912 Chester, ID	U.S. Bureau of Census 1910 U.S. census, Fremont County, Idaho; Fall River, Enumeration; Family History Library, Salt Lake City, UT Microfilm # 1374237	

- If you did not find the answer to your research objective from the source, write "No Information Found."
- If you found the answer to your research objective, write what you found.

An example of a file number system.

1 - 4/5 - 2

The first number represents the Pedigree chart number the ancestor is on. Noah Williams is on Pedigree Chart 1.

The next two numbers represent the line numbers of the husband and wife on the pedigree chart. In this case, Noah Williams is on line number 4. His wife is Elisa Munk on line number 5.

The last number is a consecutive number given to the Source Notes page, or a copy of a document, photograph, audio or video tape, etc.

Date: _15 May 1990_

Page _1_ of _2_

edigree chart number
nd/or is child number _____
ecord of (Husband's name)

File Number:

_1-4/5-2_

Page _1_

s on pedigree chart number _1_
_4_, and/or is child number _3_
group record of (Husband's name):

WILLIAMS

ay include a:
description of its
analysis of

File number
you assigned
to notes/copy
made of
information
from source

_th his wife
uildren._

_1-4/5-2_

Census

Date

Call # / Microfilm/fiche #

ource Record

mmary of results, analysis of

Research Log

Ancestor #2

Research Log

Ancestor #3

Research Log

Ancestor #4

© KBYU 2000

NOTE: In your inquiry of the source, you may have discovered information about someone or something other than the person or subject of your search. If you discovered information about one or more other persons from this source, create a new Research Log or add to an existing log for each person.

DO THIS

1. Go to the source of information.
   • Meet with the person.
   • Locate the object.
   • Find the record.

2. Investigate the source of information.
   • Interview the person and record what she/he has to say.
   • Read and make a copy of the information on the object.
   • Read and make a copy of the information on the record.

3. Write the results of your inquiry of the source on your Research Log.

MORE INFORMATION

In This Book
• How to Prepare and Conduct an Oral History Interview, page 30
• How to. . . Fill Out a Research Log, page 40
• How to Create Source Notes and Describe Information Sources, page 38

Books
• *The Everything Family Tree Book: Finding, Charting, and Preserving Your Family History,* by William G. Hartley, (Adams Media Corporation, 1998)

World Wide Web Sites
• Skillbuilding
  <www.genealogy.org/~bcg/skbld971.html>

STEP 5: Use What You Learned

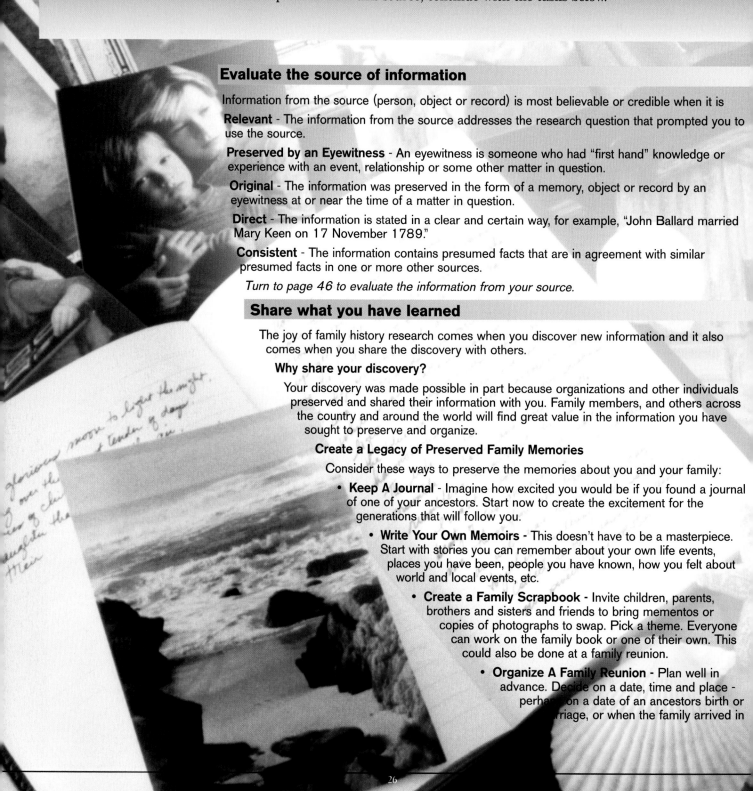

You now know whether the information source did or didn't have the answer to your research question. If the source did not have the answer, return now to step 3 on page 8 and choose a new source of information to search for the answer. If the source provided you with the information you were looking for, or if you discovered information about one or more other persons from this source, continue with the tasks below.

Evaluate the source of information

Information from the source (person, object or record) is most believable or credible when it is

Relevant - The information from the source addresses the research question that prompted you to use the source.

Preserved by an Eyewitness - An eyewitness is someone who had "first hand" knowledge or experience with an event, relationship or some other matter in question.

Original - The information was preserved in the form of a memory, object or record by an eyewitness at or near the time of a matter in question.

Direct - The information is stated in a clear and certain way, for example, "John Ballard married Mary Keen on 17 November 1789."

Consistent - The information contains presumed facts that are in agreement with similar presumed facts in one or more other sources.

Turn to page 46 to evaluate the information from your source.

Share what you have learned

The joy of family history research comes when you discover new information and it also comes when you share the discovery with others.

Why share your discovery?

Your discovery was made possible in part because organizations and other individuals preserved and shared their information with you. Family members, and others across the country and around the world will find great value in the information you have sought to preserve and organize.

Create a Legacy of Preserved Family Memories

Consider these ways to preserve the memories about you and your family:

- **Keep A Journal** - Imagine how excited you would be if you found a journal of one of your ancestors. Start now to create the excitement for the generations that will follow you.

- **Write Your Own Memoirs** - This doesn't have to be a masterpiece. Start with stories you can remember about your own life events, places you have been, people you have known, how you felt about world and local events, etc.

- **Create a Family Scrapbook** - Invite children, parents, brothers and sisters and friends to bring mementos or copies of photographs to swap. Pick a theme. Everyone can work on the family book or one of their own. This could also be done at a family reunion.

- **Organize A Family Reunion** - Plan well in advance. Decide on a date, time and place - perhaps on a date of an ancestors birth or marriage, or when the family arrived in

America. Make an agenda. Contact relatives and family friends. Ask them to bring their old photographs and share a favorite story.

- **Create An Ancestral Photo Wall** - Locate old photos of your ancestors in the possession of your relatives. Ask to make copies. Frame the photos and hang them in family groups.

- **Create A Time Capsule** - Collect photos, newspapers, a small personal item from each family member that they write about. Put them in a sealed container (there are several pre-fabricated containers available for purchase). Bury or store the container and leave clear instructions with several people or in several places about when the capsule is to be open.

- **Make an Audio Tape** - Record the voices of young and old alike at regular intervals and on special occasions.

- **Make a Family Video** - Capture the visual images. Gather old photos, mementos, and other items of value to the family or to an ancestor and videotape them. Interview and record your oldest relatives.

- **Create a Family Website** - Start your own family website. If the task seems too complex, log on to the Internet at MyFamily.com. They have made it easy to start your own website. In just minutes you can be preserving your own family information and connect with other family members around the world.

Share the Information and Memories

- **Share Information With Your Family** - Make a phone call, write a letter, discuss what you have found when you are at family gatherings, or send an e-mail with the information and photos attached .

- **Make and Share Copies Of -**
  - Pedigree Charts and Family Group Records.
  - Photos (a portrait of an ancestor, a photo of an event, building, city or a personal object that had meaning to an ancestor).
  - Stories of an ancestor's triumphs and tragedies, humor and wisdom, hardships and successes.
  - Audio and video tapes of interviews.

- **Share What You Learned To Do** - Family members can become interested when you share your discoveries about an ancestor with them. Teach them about the principles and processes of family history research that you have learned and ask them to get involved with you.

- **Share Your Information with Organizations** - Around the world, genealogical societies, public libraries with genealogical collections, and surname organizations will be very interested in your well researched genealogy, family history or biography. Join a genealogical organization or share your discoveries with other researchers with similar interests.

- **Contact Others On The Internet** - Find other genealogists on the Internet who will share their research experiences with you. Form a research network and partnership with others around the country or around the world to search together for a common ancestor.

- **Contribute Your Information To An Online Database** - You can contribute your information to an online database, such as the Ancestral File, which is part of world's largest online genealogy site, <www.FamilySearch.org>. For information to be sent to you on how to contribute your family information to Ancestral File, call 1-800-346-6044.

DO THIS

1. Evaluate the results of the search information.
   - Be careful that you do not rush to judgement about the credibility of the information that you have found.
   - Weigh all information in each piece of evidence.
   - Establish fact based on quality evidence that is clear and convincing.
   - Be continually open minded to the possibility of conflicting information.

2. Share the information with family members and others.

MORE INFORMATION

In This Book:
- How to Evaluate Evidence, page 46

In Other Books:
- Elizabeth Shown Mills, *Evidence!: Citation & Analysis for the Family Historian* (Baltimore, Maryland: Genealogical Publishing Co., 1997)
- Hartley, William G., *The Everything Family Tree Book: Finding, Charting, and Preserving Your Family History* (Holbrook, Massachusetts: Adams Media Corp., 1998)
- Hatcher, Patricia Law, *Producing a Quality Family History* (Orem, Utah: Ancestry, Inc., 1997)
- Crichton, Jennifer, Family Reunion (Workman Publishing Company, 1998)
- Slan, Joanna Campbell, *Scrapbook Storytelling: Save Family Stories and Memories With Photos, Journaling and Your Own Creativity* (Writers Digest Books, 1999)

On the World Wide Web:
- Cyndi's List of Genealogy Sites on the Internet <www.cyndislist.com>
- Along Those Lines ... "Weighing the Evidence" by George G. Morgan <www.ancestry.com/columns/george/02-12-99.htm>
- Along Those Lines ... "Joining a Genealogical or Historical Society, by George G. Morgan <www.ancestry.com/columns/george/04-10-98.htm>

SUMMARY: Steps to Discover Your Ancestors

STEP **5** **Use What You Learned**
Evaluate the results of
your inquiry and share
your information with
others.

STEP **4** **Learn From The Source**
Investigate the source for
the information you are
looking for.

STEP **3** **Choose a Source of Information**
Select a person, object or record
that may contain the information
you are looking for.

DO THIS

To discover information about the events, circumstances, relationships and background information in your ancestors' lives,

Go to step one. Write down new information you have found and organize your records.

Then, in step two, choose an ancestor. Write questions you want to answer about the ancestor on the Research Questions sheet. Choose one question at a time as your research objective. Write your research objective on a Research Log. For each ancestor you do research for, use a separate Research Log. Write all of your objectives for the same ancestor on the same log.

In step three, choose a source of information a person, an object or a record. Write your choice on the Research Log.

Next, in step four, go to the selected source of information. If the source is a person, interview the person and record it. If the source is an object or a record, read and make a copy of the information.

Finally, in step five evaluate what you have learned from the source and share any information you may have found.

Once you have finished step five, return to step one.

STEP **1** **Write Down What You Know**
Make a record of each new piece of information that you learn about an ancestor.

STEP **2** **Decide What You Want To Learn**
Focus on one ancestor at a time. Then, choose and focus on one objective at a time about a life event or background topic.

To repeat the cycle again, return to page 4

HOW TO PREPARE FOR AND CONDUCT AN ORAL HISTORY INTERVIEW

The stories and details of events and relationships in your ancestors' lives might only be discovered through an interview. Your success will of course depend on what the person can remember and how much he or she will be willing to talk about. Your success will also depend on how well you are prepared and organized. It will depend on how well you listen, how sensitive you are to feelings, and how well you are able to draw out the information you want to learn.

Plan The Interview

1. Write the question(s) about your research objective for the ancestor that you chose.

For example:
If your research objective is to learn the death date and death place of your great grandfather, you could write:

> What date (day, month and year) did great grandfather die?

> What is the name of the place (city, state, province, country) where great grandfather died?

• When you need a person to share background information and stories freely

• When you need a person to share specific facts or clarify confusing information

Ask open-ended questions, for example: What do you recall about your teenage years? How would you describe the town where you were raised? What was your father like when you grew up? What can you remember about your grandmother? What do you recall about the events surrounding her death?

Ask close-ended questions, for example: When (day, month, year) was your grandmother born? How many bothers and sisters did your father have in his family? What is your mother's maiden name? What sea port did your great aunt sail from? Where did she land when she came to America? What year?

2. Write questions about other information for the same ancestor.

For example:

> What was it like for great grandfather to work in the factory?

> How many hours did he work in a week?

> Do you remember how much he earned for one week of work?

Open - Ended Question

> Did he have to supply any of his own tools?

Close - Ended Questions

Consider writing the questions on index cards

ANCESTORS NAME: _____

QUESTION:
• Write open-ended or close-ended question here.

NOTES:
• Write brief answer to question here.
• Write rephrasing of question here.
• During the interview write questions here to follow-up on any unexpected information that is introduced.

PROPS:
• Photo, object or document to help person respond to question.

Write the number of the question here in pencil.

Question #
☐ Answered
☐ Ask again
☐ Ask follow-up

Place check mark in box:
• If question is answered.
• If question needs to be re-asked.
• If a follow-up question is needed.

3. Write questions you have about other family members.

> Ancestor #2

> Ancestor #3

Sample topics

Places where the ancestor lived (Country, state, city, neighborhood, home)

Relatives (father, mother, brothers and sisters, grandparents, aunts and uncles)

Family life (daily routines, health, activities, traditions, vacations, neighbors)

Schooling (pre-school, elementary, junior high, high school, college, trade and specialty schools)

Personal development (physical, social, spiritual, mental)

Relationships (boy-girl relations, friends during childhood, teenage, young adult and adult years, husband-wife relations, parent-child relations, other family relations, employer-employee relations)

Beliefs (personal values, political values, family values)

World and local events during lifetime (inventions, natural and man-made disasters, civil unrest, wars, fads and fashion, changes in morals, civil and human rights, jobs, climate, housing, medicine, music, etc.)

Interests, activities, and service (hobbies, talents, recreational and cultural activities, volunteer or charitable service)

HOW TO PREPARE FOR AND CONDUCT AN ORAL HISTORY INTERVIEW

Prepare for the interview

1. Organize the questions.

Start with questions that develop comfort and begin to build trust.

Place questions about sensitive topics closer to the end of the interview.

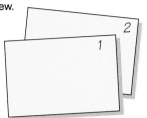

Ask an open ended question followed by one or more close ended questions on the same topic.

Place your cards in order.

- Plan the interview for no more than 1-2 hours.
- Estimate the time it will take to answer all of the questions you want to ask.
- Choose the questions you can ask in the time available.

2. Choose a method to record your interview.

Audiotape record
- Select a good quality cassette tape recorder with input hole for external microphone.
- Use high quality 60 minute tapes (30minutes per side).
- Test recorder.

Videotape record
- Plan to have at least one assistant to run a video camera while you conduct the interview.
- Use a high quality 60 minute tape.
- Test video camera.

3. Contact the person by letter or by phone.

First, if you think that you may want to publish the information from the interview, consider the need to have a written consent form signed.

Next, call or write the person and:
- Make the request for the interview (explain the purpose of interview and possible uses of information from the interview).
- Mail the questions with your letter, read the questions over the phone, or offer to send a copy of the questions.
- Explain the method you will use for recording the interview (notebook and pencil, video camera, audio tape recorder).
- As needed, get verbal agreement of willingness to sign written consent form.

Last, make an appointment (establish day, time and place) for the interview.

Conduct The Interview

1. Before interview begins:
- Remove potential distractions (phone, T.V., radio, pets, other family members, etc.).
- Record the names of the interviewer and person being interviewed, date and place of interview as a heading on the tape.

2. During interview:
- Allow for pauses to let the person finish his or her answer.
- Do not offer an opinion or interrupt answers.
- Ask follow up questions based on clues given during answers.
- When needed, ask the person from whom or how they learned the information.
- Manage tangents. Direct the person back to the subject with a rephrased question or a follow-up question.
- Manage breaks. Offer to take frequent short breaks.

3. Near end of interview:
- Get clarifications (spelling, dates, names, etc.)

Preserve The Interview

1. Label each tape
Include names of interviewer, and narrator, date, place and tape number.

2. Transcribe tape and make copies

3. Share the information
Consider giving a copy of the tape and transcription to the person you interviewed and to others.

Return to Step 1 on page 4, or Step 4 on page 24.

HOW TO GATHER AND ORGANIZE FAMILY INFORMATION

Look for and contact all possible sources of information about your family As your collection of family history records grows, organize your records for easy access. Sort and file forms and materials (such as certificates, letters, photos, awards, books, and other memorabilia) in any way that meets your needs and is convenient for you.

Gather all you can of the following from your home and the homes of relatives

Birth
- [ ] Baby Book
- [ ] Adoption Record
- [ ] Guardian Papers
- [ ] Certificate

Marriage
- [ ] Wedding Announcement
- [ ] Wedding Book
- [ ] Anniversary Announcement
- [ ] Certificate

Separation/Divorce
- [ ] Separation Papers
- [ ] Divorce Papers

Death
- [ ] Obituary
- [ ] Funeral Book
- [ ] Will
- [ ] Memorial Cards
- [ ] Certificate

School
- [ ] Report Cards
- [ ] Honor Roll
- [ ] Awards
- [ ] Graduation Diplomas
- [ ] Transcripts
- [ ] Yearbooks
- [ ] Alumni Lists
- [ ] Fraternities/Sororities

Religious Activity
- [ ] Blessing
- [ ] Baptismal Record
- [ ] Christening Record
- [ ] Confirmation Record
- [ ] Bar Mitzvah/ Bat Mitzvah
- [ ] Ordination Record
- [ ] Ministerial Record

Everyday Life
- [ ] Journal
- [ ] Diary
- [ ] Biography
- [ ] Letters
- [ ] Photographs
- [ ] Autograph Album
- [ ] Publications/ Newspaper Clippings
- [ ] Scrapbooks

- [ ] Travel Account/Log
- [ ] Achievement Award

Employment
- [ ] Social Security Card
- [ ] Apprenticeship Records Citations
- [ ] Achievement Awards
- [ ] Disability Records
- [ ] Pension Records
- [ ] Membership Records
- [ ] Income Tax Records
- [ ] Union Records
- [ ] Severance Records
- [ ] Retirement Records

Military Service
- [ ] Selective Service Records
- [ ] National Guard Service Records
- [ ] Pension Records
- [ ] Citations
- [ ] Disability Records
- [ ] Service Medals
- [ ] Ribbons
- [ ] Insignias
- [ ] Discharge Records
- [ ] Sword

- [ ] Firearms
- [ ] Uniform

Land and Property Ownership
- [ ] Deeds
- [ ] Land Grants
- [ ] Water Rights
- [ ] Mortgages
- [ ] Leases
- [ ] Tax Notices
- [ ] Abstracts of Titles
- [ ] Estate Records
- [ ] Financial Records

Civil and Legal Activity
- [ ] Bonds
- [ ] Summons
- [ ] Subpoena
- [ ] Guardian Papers
- [ ] Contracts
- [ ] Bounty Award

Family
- [ ] Bible
- [ ] Pedigree Charts

- [ ] Family Group Records
- [ ] Histories
- [ ] Bulletins/Newsletters
- [ ] Letters
- [ ] Coat of Arms

Health
- [ ] Hospital Records
- [ ] Medical Records
- [ ] Immunization Records
- [ ] X-Rays
- [ ] Insurance Papers
- [ ] Vaccination Records

Household Items
- [ ] Engraved Items
- [ ] Dishes
- [ ] Silverware
- [ ] Stitched Sampler
- [ ] Tapestries

- [ ] Quilts
- [ ] Needlework

Licenses
- [ ] Business
- [ ] Occupation
- [ ] Professional
- [ ] Hunting/Fishing
- [ ] Firearms
- [ ] Driver's
- [ ] Motor Vehicle

Citizenship Papers
- [ ] Naturalization Papers
- [ ] Alien Registration
- [ ] Deportment Papers
- [ ] Passport
- [ ] Visa

Write a letter to others to request information

Whether you telephone or write a letter to a family member, distant relative, an organization or an agency, keep your request simple and to the point.

When your write a letter:
- Provide a brief background for the reader to grasp your needs.
- Ask only a few questions at a time and write them on a separate sheet of paper with space for an answer.
- Enclose a pedigree chart or family group record for your correspondent to write in names, places and dates.4. Make your letter clean and neat in appearance.
- Send money to cover costs of photocopying, etc.
- Enclose a self-addressed, stamped envelope.
- Express your appreciation. Always acknowledge a reply.

Pedigree Chart

No. 1 on this chart is the same as
No. ____ on pedigree chart no. ____

723 First Ave.
Somewhere, U.S.A. 10523
26 February 2000

Mr. Albert Wise
553 Penn Ave
Somewhere, U.S.A. 89623

Dear Mr. Wise:

We've never met, but I understand from Kate Wright, whom I believe you know, that we're second cousins. We apparently share John Heisman as a common great-great-grandfather. My great-grandmother is Mary Ann Heisman, who was John's fourth child. I am researching my family history and am interested in obtaining information about my ancestors who lived in the Lawson Valley area. Kate told me that you have in your possession an old family Bible which may contain the information I am looking for.

I have enclosed a page with a few questions I have and space to write a response. I have also enclosed a pedigree chart with known information about my family. I would appreciate it very much if you would respond to the questions and send me a photocopy of the information in the family Bible and any other information that you feel might help me in my research.

I am enclosing a self-addressed, stamped envelope and a check for $5.00 to pay for any copying costs. If you need more money, please let me know.

I look forward to getting to know you better even if only through correspondence. If you would like to contact me by phone, my phone number is 215-555-1134. Thanks in advance for any assistance you can give me.

Sincerely,
Jennifer Tyrrell

Organize your records in a way that meets your needs and is easy to access

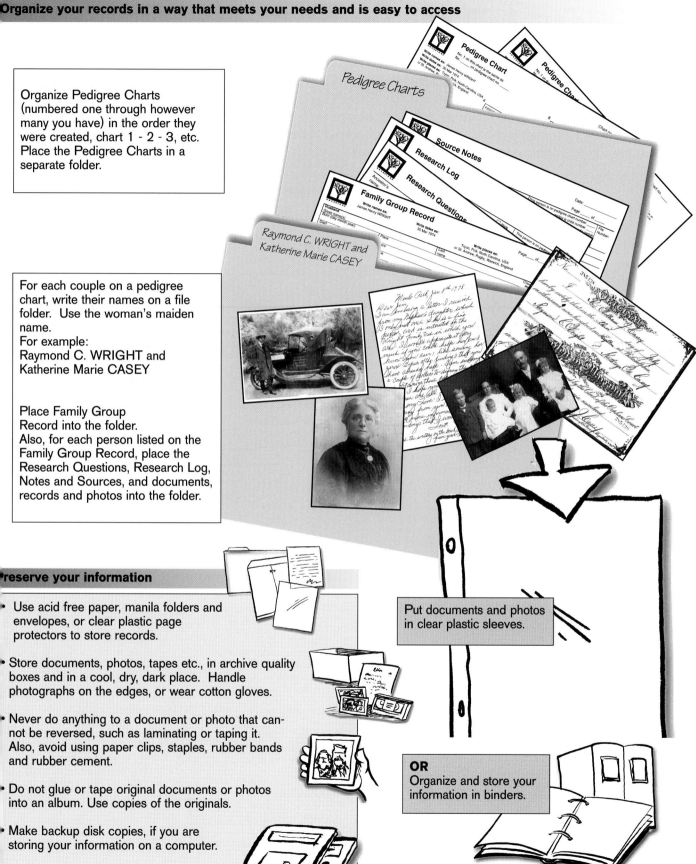

Organize Pedigree Charts (numbered one through however many you have) in the order they were created, chart 1 - 2 - 3, etc. Place the Pedigree Charts in a separate folder.

For each couple on a pedigree chart, write their names on a file folder. Use the woman's maiden name.
For example:
Raymond C. WRIGHT and
Katherine Marie CASEY

Place Family Group Record into the folder.
Also, for each person listed on the Family Group Record, place the Research Questions, Research Log, Notes and Sources, and documents, records and photos into the folder.

Preserve your information

- Use acid free paper, manila folders and envelopes, or clear plastic page protectors to store records.

- Store documents, photos, tapes etc., in archive quality boxes and in a cool, dry, dark place. Handle photographs on the edges, or wear cotton gloves.

- Never do anything to a document or photo that cannot be reversed, such as laminating or taping it. Also, avoid using paper clips, staples, rubber bands and rubber cement.

- Do not glue or tape original documents or photos into an album. Use copies of the originals.

- Make backup disk copies, if you are storing your information on a computer.

Put documents and photos in clear plastic sleeves.

OR
Organize and store your information in binders.

Return to Step 1 on page 8

WHAT TO LOOK FOR AND DO WITH THE RECORDS YOU FIND

Each record that you find may contain much more than you realize. The amount of information may be a lot to mentally process. The way in which the information is presented may be complex. There may be clues to names, dates and places. Process each presumed fact or clue one at a time. Try to use simple thinking skills.

First, look for the information that answers your research objective about your ancestor

	Clues	Presumed Facts:
A	• Mary Ellen Bright was the sister to Elizabeth.	Therefore: Elizabeth Ann Bright's mother's name was Mary Alice Thompson.
B	• Mary Ellen's mother's name was Mary Alice Thompson.	

Next, look for other information about the same ancestor

Look for dates, places, and relationships in life events.
For example, information about Elizabeth's birth.

	Clues	Presumed Facts:
		Elizabeth Ann was born on December 5th, 1902.
A	• Mary Ellen Bright was the sister to Elizabeth.	Therefore: Elizabeth Ann was born in the city of Fallbrook.
D	• (Mary Ellen's) brothers and sisters were born in the city of Fallbrook	

Then, consider information about others in the record

- **Search for other family members.** Look for direct information or clues that identify names, dates, and places about other family members. Try to establish relationships in family groups.

- **Search for others with the same surname.** Some records may contain direct information or clues about other family members with the same last name.

- **Search for multiple surnames.** The record you are searching may contain direct information or clues about relatives with a different surname.

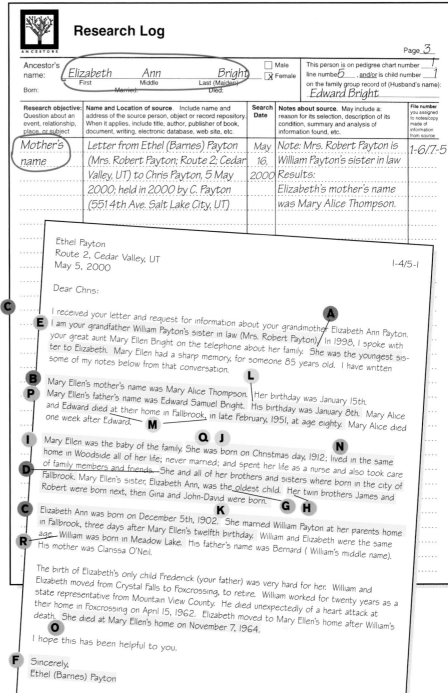

Research Log

Page 3

Ancestor's name: Elizabeth Ann Bright
First / Middle / Last (Maiden)
Born: _____ Married: _____ Died: _____

☐ Male ☒ Female

This person is on pedigree chart number 1, line number 5, and/or is child number 1 on the family group record of (Husband's name): Edward Bright

Research objective: Question about an event, relationship, place, or subject	Name and Location of source. Include name and address of the source person, object or record repository. When it applies, include title, author, publisher of book, document, writing, electronic database, web site, etc.	Search Date	Notes about source. May include a: reason for its selection, description of its condition, summary and analysis of information found, etc.	File number you assigned to notes/copy made of information from source
Mother's name	Letter from Ethel (Barnes) Payton (Mrs. Robert Payton; Route 2; Cedar Valley, UT) to Chris Payton, 5 May 2000; held in 2000 by C. Payton (551 4th Ave. Salt Lake City, UT)	May 16, 2000	Note: Mrs. Robert Payton is William Payton's sister in law Results: Elizabeth's mother's name was Mary Alice Thompson.	1-6/.7-5

Ethel Payton
Route 2, Cedar Valley, UT
May 5, 2000   1-4/5-1

Dear Chris:

I received your letter and request for information about your grandmother Elizabeth Ann Payton. I am your grandfather William Payton's sister in law (Mrs. Robert Payton). In 1998, I spoke with your great aunt Mary Ellen Bright on the telephone about her family. She was the youngest sister to Elizabeth. Mary Ellen had a sharp memory, for someone 85 years old. I have written some of my notes below from that conversation.

Mary Ellen's mother's name was Mary Alice Thompson. Her birthday was January 15th. Mary Ellen's father's name was Edward Samuel Bright. His birthday was January 8th. Mary Alice and Edward died at their home in Fallbrook, in late February, 1951, at age eighty. Mary Alice died one week after Edward.

Mary Ellen was the baby of the family. She was born on Christmas day, 1912; lived in the same home in Woodside all of her life; never married; and spent her life as a nurse and also took care of family members and friends. She and all of her brothers and sisters where born in the city of Fallbrook. Mary Ellen's sister, Elizabeth Ann, was the oldest child. Her twin brothers James and Robert were born next, then Gina and John-David were born.

Elizabeth Ann was born on December 5th, 1902. She married William Payton at her parents home in Fallbrook, three days after Mary Ellen's twelfth birthday. William and Elizabeth were the same age. William was born in Meadow Lake. His father's name was Bernard (William's middle name). His mother was Clarissa O'Neil.

The birth of Elizabeth's only child Frederick (your father) was very hard for her. William and Elizabeth moved from Crystal Falls to Foxcrossing, to retire. William worked for twenty years as a state representative from Mountain View County. He died unexpectedly of a heart attack at their home in Foxcrossing on April 15, 1962. Elizabeth moved to Mary Ellen's home after William's death. She died at Mary Ellen's home on November 7, 1964.

I hope this has been helpful to you.

Sincerely,
Ethel (Barnes) Payton

Extract relevant information from each record

Identify names and establish relationships between individuals

Example: Identify Mary Ellen's father's name

Mary Ellen's father's name was Edward Samuel Bright.

Research Log
Edward Samuel Bright

Example: Establish that William Payton had a brother Robert and sister-in-law Ethel

Clues	Presumed Facts:
• I am your grandfather William Payton's sister-in-law (Mrs. Robert Payton) • Sincerely, Ethel (Barnes) Payton	Therefore: 1. William has a brother Robert. 2. Robert has a wife Ethel, with a maiden name of Barnes.

Research Log
Ethel Barnes — G

Research Log
William Payton — H

Research Log
William Payton — I

OR

Example: Establish the birth order of Edward Samuel Bright and Mary Alice Thompson's children.

Clues	Presumed Facts:
• Elizabeth Ann was the oldest child. • Her twin brothers James and Robert were born next, then Gina and John-David • Mary Ellen was the baby of the family	Therefore: The birth order is: 1. Elizabeth Ann 2. James 3. Robert 4. Gina 5. John-David 6. Mary Ellen

Research Log
Edward Samuel Bright

Research Log
Elizabeth A. Bright

Research Log
James Bright

Research Log
Robert Bright

Research Log
Gina Bright

Research Log
John-David Bright

Research Log
Mary Ellen Bright

Identify, calculate and approximate dates

Example: Identify Mary Ellen's birth date

• (Mary Ellen) was born on Christmas day, 1912

Research Log
Mary Ellen Bright

Example: Calculate the date of marriage between William Payton and Elizabeth Ann Bright

Clues	Presumed Facts:
• (Mary Ellen) was born on Christmas day, 1912 • (Elizabeth Ann) married William Payton. . . three days after Mary Ellen's twelfth birthday.	Therefore: William and Elizabeth were married on December 28, 1924.

Calculation:		
Christmas day	(Dec. 25)	1912
+ Mary Ellen's Age		12
+ Birthday	3 days	
=	Dec. 28	1924

Research Log
Elizabeth A. Bright — L

Research Log
William Payton — M

Example: Approximate the date of birth of Edward Samuel Bright

Clues	Presumed Facts:
• Edward Samuel Bright's birthday was January 8th. • Edward died... in late February 1951, at age eighty.	Therefore: Edward was born on January 8, in approximately 1871.

Calculation:	
Death year:	1951
- Years lived:	80
= (approx. birth year)	1871

Research Log
Edward Samuel Bright

Identify and derive the names of places

Example: Identify the place where William Payton was born.

William was born in Meadow Lake

Research Log
William Payton

Example: Establish that William Payton had a brother Robert and sister-in-law Ethel

Clues	Presumed Facts:
• (Mary Ellen) lived in the same home in Woodside all of her life • (Elizabeth Ann) died at Mary Ellen's home...	Therefore: Elizabeth Ann died in Woodside.

Research Log
Elizabeth A. Bright

Return to Step 1 on page 4 or Step 4 on page 24

HOW TO FILL OUT A PEDIGREE CHART AND FAMILY GROUP RECORD

Use a Pedigree Chart to write information about you, your parents, grandparents and other direct line ancestors. Use a separate Family Group Record to record information about each couple on the Pedigree Chart, and other couples with children.

Fill Out A Pedigree Chart

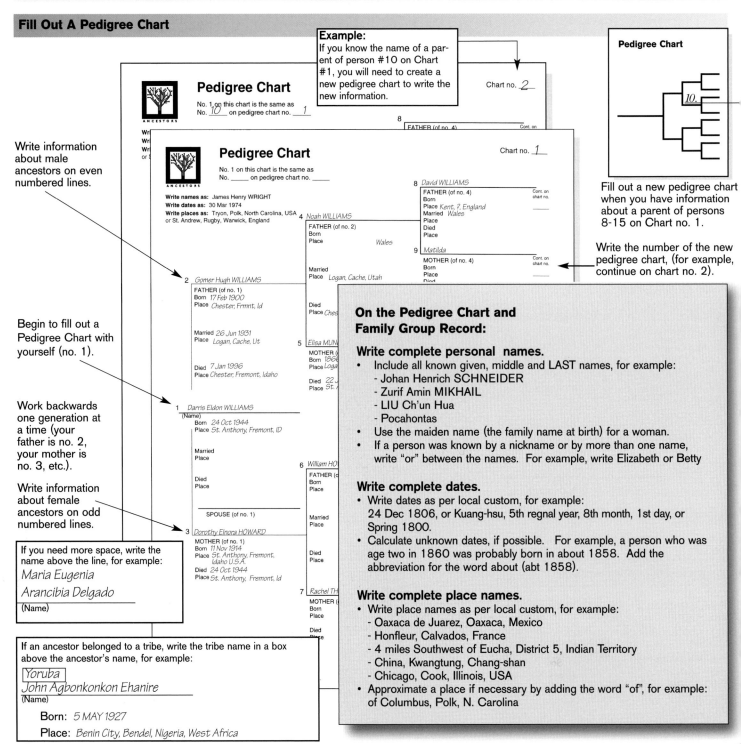

Example:
If you know the name of a parent of person #10 on Chart #1, you will need to create a new pedigree chart to write the new information.

Pedigree Chart

Fill out a new pedigree chart when you have information about a parent of persons 8-15 on Chart no. 1.

Write the number of the new pedigree chart, (for example, continue on chart no. 2).

Write information about male ancestors on even numbered lines.

Begin to fill out a Pedigree Chart with yourself (no. 1).

Work backwards one generation at a time (your father is no. 2, your mother is no. 3, etc.).

Write information about female ancestors on odd numbered lines.

If you need more space, write the name above the line, for example:
Maria Eugenia Arancibia Delgado
(Name)

If an ancestor belonged to a tribe, write the tribe name in a box above the ancestor's name, for example:
Yoruba
John Agbonkonkon Ehanire
(Name)
Born: *5 MAY 1927*
Place: *Benin City, Bendel, Nigeria, West Africa*

On the Pedigree Chart and Family Group Record:

Write complete personal names.
- Include all known given, middle and LAST names, for example:
  - Johan Henrich SCHNEIDER
  - Zurif Amin MIKHAIL
  - LIU Ch'un Hua
  - Pocahontas
- Use the maiden name (the family name at birth) for a woman.
- If a person was known by a nickname or by more than one name, write "or" between the names. For example, write Elizabeth or Betty

Write complete dates.
- Write dates as per local custom, for example:
  24 Dec 1806, or Kuang-hsu, 5th regnal year, 8th month, 1st day, or Spring 1800.
- Calculate unknown dates, if possible. For example, a person who was age two in 1860 was probably born in about 1858. Add the abbreviation for the word about (abt 1858).

Write complete place names.
- Write place names as per local custom, for example:
  - Oaxaca de Juarez, Oaxaca, Mexico
  - Honfleur, Calvados, France
  - 4 miles Southwest of Eucha, District 5, Indian Territory
  - China, Kwangtung, Chang-shan
  - Chicago, Cook, Illinois, USA
- Approximate a place if necessary by adding the word "of", for example:
  of Columbus, Polk, N. Carolina

Fill Out A Family Group Record

Write the name of the father (next to Husband) and mother (next to Wife), and their biological and/or adopted children (in order of birth).

NOTE: If there are children from another marriage, fill out a separate Family Group Record and list the father, mother, and children of that marriage.

Person Number 1 on this chart is the same as no. 10 on chart no. 1

CHART #2

Check the box for male or female

Write the names of the parents of #10 on lines two and three of the new chart.

On line #1 of your new chart, rewrite the name of person #10 from pedigree chart #1.

List the spouse(s) of other marriage(s) on the back of the Family Group Record.

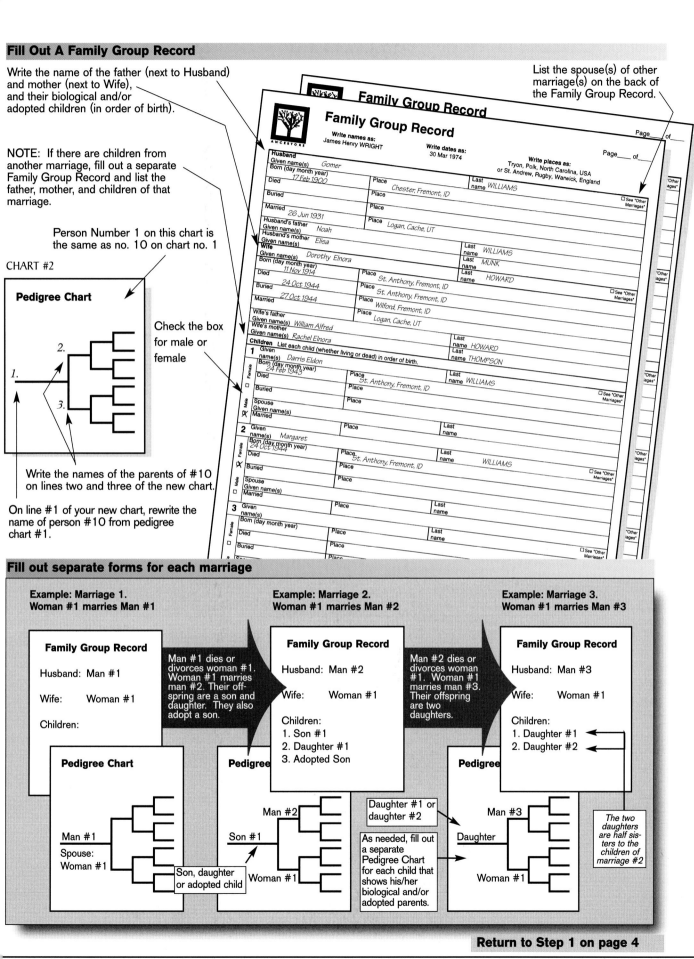

Fill out separate forms for each marriage

Example: Marriage 1.
Woman #1 marries Man #1

Family Group Record

Husband: Man #1

Wife: Woman #1

Children:

Man #1 dies or divorces woman #1. Woman #1 marries man #2. Their offspring are a son and daughter. They also adopt a son.

Example: Marriage 2.
Woman #1 marries Man #2

Family Group Record

Husband: Man #2

Wife: Woman #1

Children:
1. Son #1
2. Daughter #1
3. Adopted Son

Man #2 dies or divorces woman #1. Woman #1 marries man #3. Their offspring are two daughters.

Example: Marriage 3.
Woman #1 marries Man #3

Family Group Record

Husband: Man #3

Wife: Woman #1

Children:
1. Daughter #1
2. Daughter #2

Pedigree Chart

Man #1
Spouse:
Woman #1

Son, daughter or adopted child

Pedigree

Son #1

Man #2

Woman #1

Daughter #1 or daughter #2

As needed, fill out a separate Pedigree Chart for each child that shows his/her biological and/or adopted parents.

Pedigree

Daughter

Man #3

Woman #1

The two daughters are half sisters to the children of marriage #2

Return to Step 1 on page 4

How To Create Source Notes
and Describe Information Sources

Family members and others will be interested to know where you found each piece of information about an ancestor. Use the Source Notes form to record information that you discover about an ancestor from a person, object or record. Describe each source in detail.

Record information from a source person, object or record

Source Person

1. Place a check in the box to indicate if the source is a person, object or record. Then fill in the information about the person, object or record.

2. Write information learned from the source.

3. Place a check mark in the box next to each event, relationship, description, place, etc. to summarize information obtained from the source person, object or record.

Source Object

Identify the Pedigree Chart and/or Family Group Record this ancestor appears on.

Write the file number that you want to assign to these source notes.

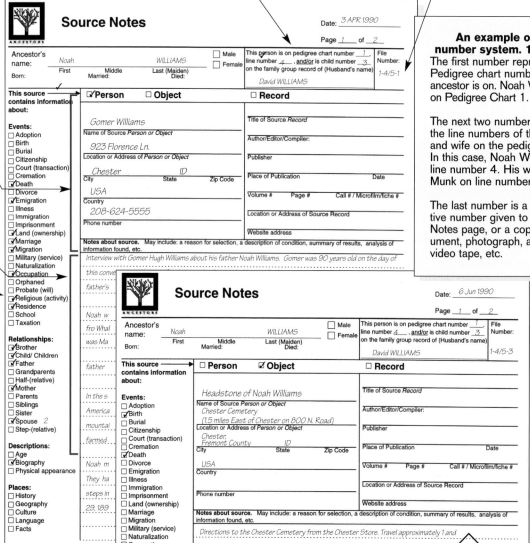

Source Notes

Date: 3 APR 1990

Page 1 of 2

Ancestor's name: Noah / WILLIAMS — First / Middle / Last (Maiden)
☐ Male ☑ Female
Born: / Married: / Died:

This person is on pedigree chart number 1, line number 4, and/or is child number 3 on the family group record of (Husband's name) David WILLIAMS

File Number: 1-4/5-1

This source contains information about:

☑ Person ☐ Object ☐ Record

Gomer Williams
Name of Source Person or Object

923 Florence Ln.
Location or Address of Person or Object

Chester   ID
City   State   Zip Code

USA
Country

208-624-5555
Phone number

Events:
☐ Adoption
☐ Birth
☐ Burial
☐ Citizenship
☐ Court (transaction)
☐ Cremation
☑ Death
☐ Divorce
☑ Emigration
☐ Illness
☐ Immigration
☐ Imprisonment
☑ Land (ownership)
☑ Marriage
☑ Migration
☐ Military (service)
☐ Naturalization
☑ Occupation
☐ Orphaned
☐ Probate (will)
☑ Religious (activity)
☑ Residence
☐ School
☐ Taxation

Relationships:
☑ Brother
☑ Child/ Children
☑ Father
☐ Grandparents
☐ Half-(relative)
☑ Mother
☐ Parents
☐ Siblings
☐ Sister
☑ Spouse 2
☐ Step-(relative)

Descriptions:
☐ Age
☑ Biography
☐ Physical appearance

Places:
☐ History
☐ Geography
☐ Culture
☐ Language
☐ Facts

Permission is granted to copy this form for personal use

Title of Source Record

Author/Editor/Compiler:

Publisher

Place of Publication   Date

Volume #   Page #   Call # / Microfilm/fiche #

Location or Address of Source Record

Website address

Notes about source. May include: a reason for selection, a description of condition, summary of results, analysis of information found, etc.

Interview with Gomer Hugh Williams about his father Noah Williams. Gomer was 90 years old on the day of this conve...
father's
Noah w
fro Whal
was Ma
father
In the s
America
mountai
farmed
Noah m
They ha
steps in
29, 189

An example of a file number system. 1 - 4/5 - The first number represents th Pedigree chart number the ancestor is on. Noah Williams is on Pedigree Chart 1.

The next two numbers represe the line numbers of the husba and wife on the pedigree char In this case, Noah Williams is line number 4. His wife is Elis Munk on line number 5.

The last number is a consecu-tive number given to the Sour Notes page, or a copy of a doc ument, photograph, audio or video tape, etc.

Source Notes

Date: 6 Jun 1990

Page 1 of 2

Ancestor's name: Noah / WILLIAMS — First / Middle / Last (Maiden)
☐ Male ☑ Female
Born: / Married: / Died:

This person is on pedigree chart number 1, line number 4, and/or is child number 3 on the family group record of (Husband's name) David WILLIAMS

File Number: 1-4/5-3

This source contains information about:

☐ Person ☑ Object ☐ Record

Headstone of Noah Williams
Name of Source Person or Object

Chester Cemetery
(1.5 miles East of Chester on 800 N. Road)
Location or Address of Person or Object

Chester,
Fremont County   ID
City   State   Zip Code

USA
Country

Phone number

Events:
☐ Adoption
☑ Birth
☐ Burial
☐ Citizenship
☐ Court (transaction)
☐ Cremation
☑ Death
☐ Divorce
☐ Emigration
☐ Illness
☐ Immigration
☐ Imprisonment
☐ Land (ownership)
☐ Marriage
☐ Migration
☐ Military (service)
☐ Naturalization
☐ Occupation
☐ Orphaned
☐ Probate (will)
☐ Religious (activity)
☐ Residence
☐ School
☐ Taxation

Relationships:
☐ Brother

Title of Source Record

Author/Editor/Compiler:

Publisher

Place of Publication   Date

Volume #   Page #   Call # / Microfilm/fiche #

Location or Address of Source Record

Website address

Notes about source. May include: a reason for selection, a description of condition, summary of results, analysis of information found, etc.

Directions to the Chester Cemetery from the Chester Store. Travel approximately 1 and
1/2 miles East from the Chester Store on 800 North Road. Cross the canal bridge,
turn right and cross the cattle guard. Follow the dirt lane West along the canal
to the foot path entrance to the cemetery.
Location of burial plat and headstone:
From the entrance to the cemetery the head

Noah Williams
26 JAN 1853 - JUN 1914
"Weep not for he is at rest".

Source Record

Source Notes

Date: *15 May 1990*

Page *1* of *2*

Ancestor's name: *Noah* / *WILLIAMS*
First / Middle / Last (Maiden)
Born: / Married: / Died:

☑ Male ☐ Female

This person is on pedigree chart number *1*, line number *4*, **and/or** is child number *3* on the family group record of (Husband's name) *David WILLIAMS*

File Number: *1-4/5-2*

This source contains information about:

☐ Person ☐ Object ☑ Record

Idaho, 1910 Federal Census
Title of Source Record
U.S. Bureau of Census
Author/Editor/Compiler:
National Archives
Publisher
Washington, D.C.
Place of Publication / Date *1374237*
Volume # / Page # / Call # / Microfilm/fiche #
Family History Library
Location or Address of Source Record
Website address

Events:
☐ Adoption
☑ Birth
☐ Burial
☑ Citizenship
☐ Court (transaction)
☐ Cremation
☐ Death
☐ Divorce
☑ Emigration
☐ Illness
☐ Immigration
☐ Imprisonment
☐ Land (ownership)
☑ Marriage
☐ Migration
☐ Military (service)
☐ Naturalization
☑ Occupation
☐ Orphaned
☐ Probate (will)
☐ Religious (activity)
☐ Residence
☐ School
☐ Taxation

Name of Source Person or Object
Location or Address of Person or Object
City / State / Zip Code
Country
Phone number

Notes about source. May include: a reason for selection, a description of condition, summary of results, analysis of information found, etc.

Noah Williams is listed with his wife Eliza and eight children.
Fremont County, Idaho; Fall River Precinct, Enumeration District [ED] 132,
Supervisor District [SD] 46; sheet #5a, dwelling #53, family #64;
Noah's father and mother were born in Wales. Eliza's father and mother were born in
Denmark.

Relationships:
☐ Brother
☑ Child/ Children
☑ Father
☐ Grandparents
☐ Half-(relative)
☑ Mother
☐ Parents
☐ Siblings
☐ Sister
☑ Spouse
☐ Step-(relative)

Name	Relationship to head of Family	Age	Birthplace
Noah	Head	58	Wales
Eliza	Wife	44	Utah
Blodwen	Dau	16	Utah
Gladys	Dau	15	Idaho
Trevor N.	Son	13	Idaho
Gomer H.	Son	10	Idaho

Write complete information sources

When you describe your sources on your Research Log, write complete source information. For example:

Name of source person / Address of source person / Person conducting interview / Date and place of interview

Gomer Williams, 923 Florence Ln, Chester, ID, USA, Interviewed by Daris Williams, 3 Apr 1990 at Chester, ID, USA; audio tape and notes in possession of Daris Williams, 374 Ventnor Ave., Denver, CO, USA.

Format of recorded information (Example: notes, audio/video tape) / Person in possession of recorded information / Location of recorded information

Name of source object / Address of source object

Gravestone; Chester Cemetery, Chester, Fremont County, ID, USA, (1.5 Miles East of Chester on 800 N. Road); Notes and photograph made 6 Jun 1990 by Daris Williams; 374 Ventnor Ave., Denver, CO, USA.

Format of recorded information (Example: notes, audio/video tape, photograph) / Date object was seen and information was recorded / Person who saw object and recorded information / Location of recorded information

Author of record / Title of source record / Year(s) covered in record source

U.S. Bureau of Census, 1910 U.S. census, Fremont County, Idaho; Fall River Precinct, Enumeration District [ED] 132, Supervisor District [SD] 46; sheet #5a, dwelling #53, family #64; Family History Library, Salt Lake City, UT microfilm #1374237

Specific reference / Location of record source

Return to Step 1 on page 4 or Step 4 on page 24

HOW TO WRITE RESEARCH QUESTIONS AND FILL OUT A RESEARCH LOG

Use the Research Questions form to write questions you have about the event dates and places, relationships and circumstances of an ancestor's life. Then, use a Research Log to focus on one question at a time about the same ancestor. Your Research Log will keep your research focused and remind you of information sources that you have contacted or searched.

Look for missing and unverified information

Look at the missing or unverified information on the Pedigree Chart, Family Group Record and Source Notes about the ancestor you chose.

Write questions you want to answer

Use the Research Questions form and write a question about each missing or unverified piece of information.

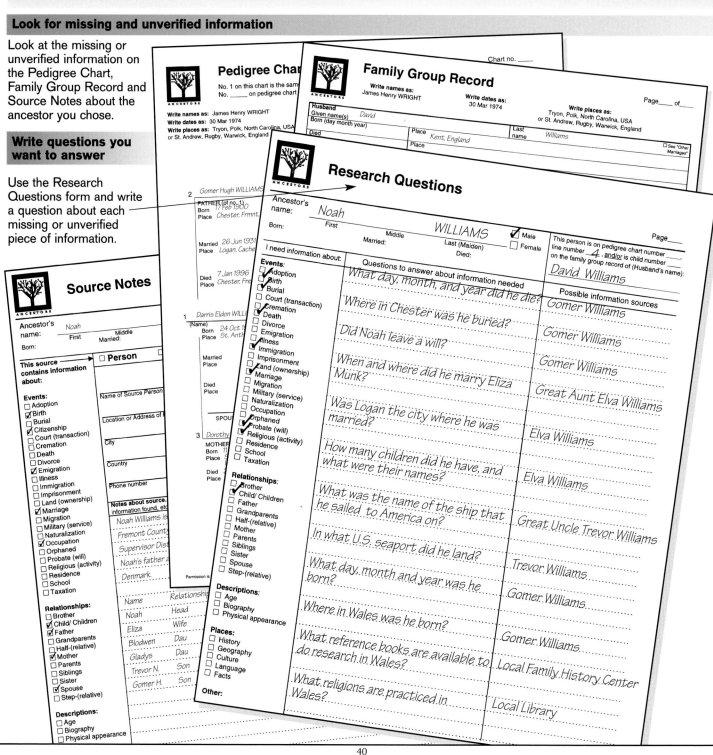

Write one question at a time on the research log

Identify the Pedigree Chart and/or Family Group Record this ancestor appears on.

Fill out this information as part of Step 2.

- Ancestor's name and sex
- Known dates and places of birth, marriage and death to refer to while doing research
- Research objective - an abbreviated form of a question that contains clues or approximations to answer the question.

Example:
Death Date
Chester, Idaho?
Abt. 1912?

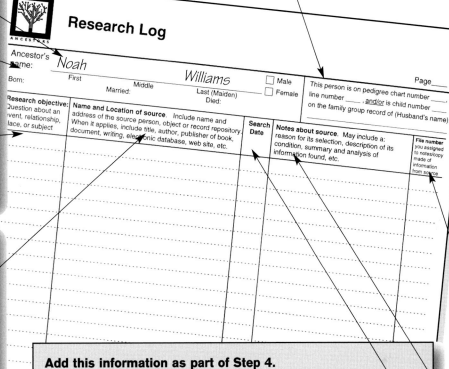

Research Log

Ancestor's Name: *Noah* *Williams*
First   Middle   Last (Maiden)
Born:
Married:
Died:
☐ Male   ☐ Female

Page____

This person is on pedigree chart number ____, line number ____, and/or is child number ____ on the family group record of (Husband's name):

Research objective: Question about an event, relationship, place, or subject

Name and Location of source. Include name and address of the source person, object or record repository. When it applies, include title, author, publisher of book, document, writing, electronic database, web site, etc.

Search Date

Notes about source. May include a: reason for its selection, description of its condition, summary and analysis of information found, etc.

File number you assigned to notes/copy made of information from source.

Add this information as part of Step 3.

- A complete name, address and description of the information source.

Example for a Source Person:
Gomer Williams, 923 Florence Ln, Chester, ID, USA, Interviewed by Daris Williams, 3 Apr 1990 at Chester, ID, USA; audio tape and notes in possession of Daris Williams, 374 Ventnor Ave., Denver, CO, USA.

Example for a Source Object:
Gravestone; Chester Cemetery, Chester, Fremont County, ID, USA, (1.5 Miles East of Chester on 800 N. Road); Notes and photograph made 6 Jun 1990 by Daris Williams; 374 Ventnor Ave., Denver, CO, USA.

Example for a Source Record:
U.S. Bureau of Census, 1910 U.S. census, Fremont County, Idaho; Fall River Precinct, Enumeration District [ED] 132, Supervisor District [SD] 46; sheet #5a, dwelling #53, family #64; Family History Library, Salt Lake City, UT microfilm #1374237

Note: For more information on how to describe information sources, see How To Create Notes and Describe Information Sources on page 38.

Add this information as part of Step 4.

- The date that you actually saw or heard the information from the source.
- Notes about the information from the source.
  Consider making notes about any these:
  - A reason for selecting the source.
  - A description of the condition of the source.
    Describe the physical condition of an object or record and the ease or difficulty of reading the information. Describe the mental state of mind of a person and his/her ability to recall and clearly present facts and feelings.
  - A summary of the information found. If you did not find the information you were seeking, write "No information found." If you did find information about your objective, write enough information to give evidence that the objective has been accomplished.
  - An analysis of the information found. State any questions or conclusions you may have. Also, state the reasons for any conclusions.
- A file number you assigned to the notes, audio and/or video recording, or copy of the information you found.

Note: For more information on file numbers, see "How to Create Notes and Describe Information Sources" on page 38.

Return to: Step 2 on page, 6 Step 3 on page 10, or Step 4 on page 24

UNDERSTAND AND USE
THE WORLD OF INFORMATION

Around the World

1. In your ancestors' lives, events happened.

Your ancestors were born and have died, or someday will die. Between the events of birth and death, any number of other events may have taken place in their lives.

8. Find the best information about your ancestors.

The best information sources are:
- Relevant (related to what you want to learn about your ancestors).
- Original (information about an event, relationship or circumstance was preserved at the time it happened).
- Direct (clear and certain about the presumed facts they contain).
- Eyewitnesses who are trustworthy.
- Consistent with other sources about the same information.

7. Original and compiled information is usually stored somewhere within the jurisdiction where it was created.

- If information is preserved in the mind of someone, that person is a moving storage place.

- If information is preserved in a written record, the record may be in a home, courthouse, library, archive or any other place where records and documents are stored.

- If information is preserved in an object, the object may or may not be in the jurisdiction where it was created.

6. Presumed fact is preserved in original and compiled information sources.

- Information preserved by an eyewitness at the time of an event is considered original information.

- Information preserved by a hearsay witness is considered compiled information.

- Compiled information is often easiest to find. However, original information is the best source of information.

UNDERSTAND AND USE THE WORLD OF INFORMATION

Events happened within various country jurisdictions.

A jurisdiction is the territory within which authority may be exercised. An ancestor may have lived within several jurisdictions.

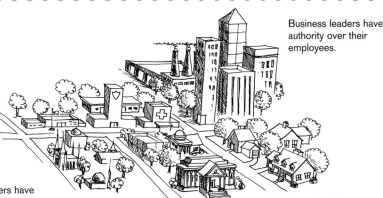

Business leaders have authority over their employees.

Institutional leaders have authority over their patrons.

Religious leaders have authority over their congregations.

Government leaders have authority over people within the jurisdictions of nations, provinces, states, counties, cities, towns, villages, and tribes.

The family is at the core of all jurisdictions. Parents have authority over their children.

3. Wherever your ancestors lived, authorities and individuals preserved information in various forms.

Depending on the culture, information about certain events may have been preserved in the form of a memory, an object, or written record.

4. Each form of information was created by an eyewitness or a hearsay witness.

An eyewitness is someone who saw an event and then made a mental note, a written note or an object containing information about the event.

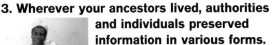

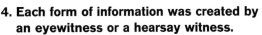

yewitnesses and hearsay witnesses stify of presumed fact.

A fact about a person is information that is true and accurate about that person's name, a date, place, event, relationship and/or circumstance. Think of the information contained in a source (a person's memory, or a written record, or an object) as presumed fact, until you prove the information to be true and accurate.

A hearsay witness is someone who made a mental note, a written note or an object, based on the account of an eyewitness or another hearsay witness.

Return to STEP 1 on pg. 8, or STEP 3 on pg. 12

HOW THE INTERNET WORKS AND WHERE TO SEARCH

The largest computer system in the world is known as the Internet. Government agencies, colleges, businesses, organizations and individuals connect their computers to the Internet, and become part of a worldwide network. When you are connected to the Internet, you can access information on any subject on the World Wide Web, exchange electronic mail (e-mail) and join a discussion group to meet people with similar interests.

The World Wide Web, also called the Web, is made up of Websites

A Website can be created and maintained by an individual, family, business, college, government agency, etc.

A Website is like a book. It has a title page and one or more Web pages

The first page of a Website is called the Home Page. Just like the address where you live is unique in all of the world, each Web page has an address that is unique in all of the world. The address is called a Uniform Resource Locator or URL. If you know a URL, you can view a Web page anywhere in the world.
For example: www.cyndislist.com

A Web page can be linked to any other Web pages

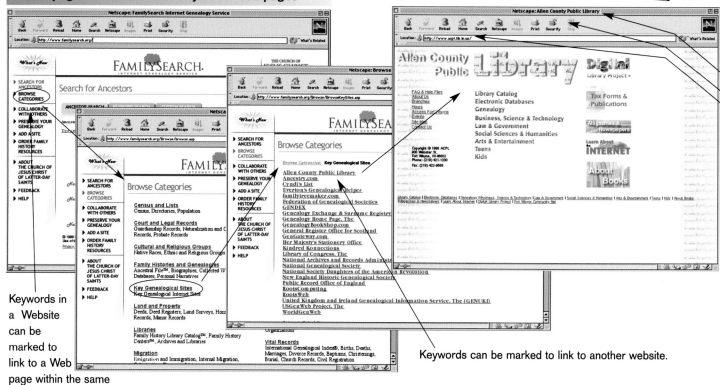

Keywords in a Website can be marked to link to a Web page within the same Website.

Keywords can be marked to link to another website.

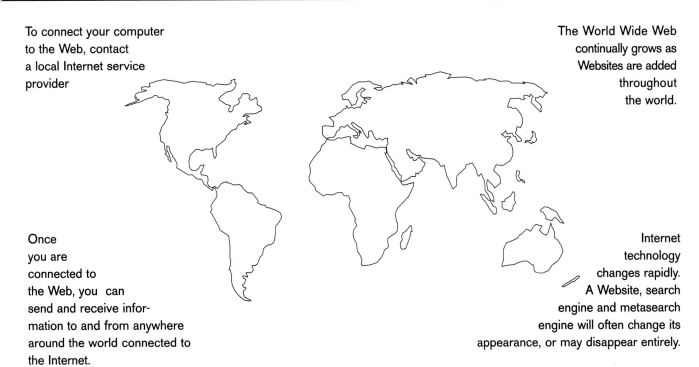

To connect your computer to the Web, contact a local Internet service provider

The World Wide Web continually grows as Websites are added throughout the world.

Once you are connected to the Web, you can send and receive information to and from anywhere around the world connected to the Internet.

Internet technology changes rapidly. A Website, search engine and metasearch engine will often change its appearance, or may disappear entirely.

Use the Internet to send and receive electronic mail

E-mail or electronic mail is a valuable tool to use for family history research. Send (e-mail) to anyone connected to the Internet around the world.

Use the Internet to join a discussion group

Join a discussion group to meet people with similar family history interests. Ask questions and discuss research problems with other researchers around the world.

Each Web page can be viewed on your computer using a Web browser

Your Web browser will display a:
• Menu bar
• Toolbar of buttons used to perform common tasks
• URL address of the Web page

When the Web page is located, it will appear in the Web browser's display window.

Use a search engine to locate the type of information that you are looking for

A search engine looks for keywords on selected Websites. Some search engines focus on particular subjects or geographic locations. Other search engines will focus on specialized Websites. No one search engine searches all of the sites on the Web. However, some search engines called metasearch engines actually conduct searches of search engines.

How to use the Internet

Learn how to: surf the net, use E-mail, find information fast, download files from the Internet to your personal computer, join newsgroups, build a website and more.

The sites listed below will teach you to master the basics of Internet use. On your web browser URL address line, type the web address enclosed in the <angle brackets>.

Learn The Net
<www.learnthenet.com>

Help-2-Go
<www.help2go.com/BestoftheNet/index.cfm>

Navigating the World Wide Web
<www.imaginarylandscape.com/helpweb/www/www.html>

ThirdAge
<www.thirdage.com/features/tech/booster/>

Beginners Central
<http://northernwebs.com/bc/>

Creative Good
<www.creativegood.com/help/index.html>

Newbie dot Org

Return to Step 3 on page 22

HOW THE INTERNET WORKS AND WHERE TO SEARCH

HOW TO EVALUATE EVIDENCE

In family history research, evidence is the information that a source (person, object or record) provides as truth or fact. The information that you found may be truthful, accurate and what you believe to be a fact. You will need to judge how credible the information is in each source. Then, you will need to weigh all of the evidence you have found about the matter in question.

Determine if the information from the source is relevant

1. Irrelevance vs. Relevance

Is the information within the source relevant? Does it address the specific matter in question that prompted you to use the source?

	Recommended Action to Take
☐ **YES**. The information is relevant.	Answer questions 2-7 below.
☐ **NO**. The information is irrelevant.	Return to page 8 and choose another source.

Determine the degree of credibility of the information from the source

2. Hearsay Witness vs. Eyewitness

Does the relevant information appear to have been preserved by a hearsay witness?

☐ **YES**. A "hearsay witness." The information was preserved by someone who heard or saw information from an eyewitness or another hearsay witness.

☐ **NO**. An "eyewitness." The information was preserved by someone who had first hand knowledge or experience with the matter in question.

3. Indirectness vs. Directness of Information

Is the information stated indirectly in a way that you must apply a thought process to make a conclusion about the matter in question?

☐ **YES**. Indirectly The information is stated in an unclear or uncertain way, for example, "In November, 1790, John Ballard and Mary Keen had been married for about one year."

☐ **NO**. Directly. The information is stated in a clear and certain way, for example, "John Ballard married Mary Keen on 17 November 1789."

4. Compiled or Copied vs. Original Information

Do you have any reason to believe that the information you found may have been compiled (a duplicated or transcribed copy, or a retold version from an original source)?

☐ **YES**. Compiled. The information was preserved by someone who heard or saw information from an eyewitness or another hearsay witness.

☐ **NO**. Original. The information is from a memory, object or record that was preserved by an eyewitness at or near the time of the matter in question.

5. Trustworthiness and Ability of Informant, Scribe, and Custodian of the Information

Do you have any reason to believe that either the informant, scribe, or custodian altered the information or lacked the knowledge, skill or alert frame of mind to clearly and accurately preserve the information you found?

☐ **YES**. One or more was not trustworthy and/or lacked the knowledge, skill or an alert frame of mind.

☐ **NO**. All were trustworthy and had the knowledge, skill and alert frame of mind.

6. Time When Information Was Preserved

Do you have any reason to believe that the information was preserved much later than "at or near the time" the matter in question occurred?

☐ **YES**. The information was preserved much later than the time of the matter in question.

☐ **NO**. The information was preserved "at or near the time" of the matter in question.

7. Incompleteness vs. Completeness of Information

Does the information within the source incompletely address the matter in question?

☐ **YES**. The information was incomplete in addressing all parts of the matter in question.

☐ **NO**. The information was complete in addressing all parts of the matter in question.

For questions 2-7, add the number you answered with a "No." Then, note the number, level of credibility and action to take.

Number of questions answered with a "NO"	Level of credibility of the source information	Recommended action to take
0 - 2 with a "NO" answer	This information appears to have a **low level of credibility.**	Return to page 8 and choose another source to answer your research objective.
3 - 4 with a "NO" answer	This information appears to have **some level of credibility.**	Go to question eight and determine the consistency of this source information.
5 - 6 with a "NO" answer	This information appears to have **a high level of credibility.**	Go to question eight and determine the consistency of this source information.

Determine the consistency of the source information

8 — Inconsistency vs. Consistency of Information

Is the information within the source consistent with other information you have gathered concerning the matter in question?

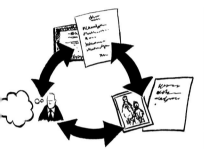

	Recommended Action to Take
☐ **NO INFORMATION TO COMPARE WITH**. At present, I have not gathered information from any other source about the same matter in question.	Return to page 8 and choose another source to validate the information you found about the matter in question.
☐ **NO.** The information is inconsistent with other known information sources about the same matter in question.	Return to page 8 and choose another source to validate the information you found about the matter in question.
☐ **YES.** The information is consistent with other known information sources about the same matter in question.	Determine the quality of the information in all sources about the matter in question.

Determine the quality of the evidence

9 — Quality vs. Quality of Evidence

Do you believe that the quality of the information you found to answer your research objective suggests a reasonable conclusion of fact about the matter in question?

	Recommended Action to Take
☐ **NO.** The quality of evidence is insufficient to reach a reasonable conclusion of fact about the matter in question.	Return to page 8 and choose another source to validate the information you found about the matter in question.
☐ **YES.** The quality of evidence is sufficient to reach a reasonable conclusion of fact about the matter in question	Record your conclusions on your Research Log. Then, return to Step 1 on page 8, or Step 5 on page 30.

Fact is information that truthfully and accurately represents a person as he or she was or an event, relationship or circumstance as it actually happened.

Until you can reasonably conclude some fact(s) about the matter in question from all of the evidence, you should think of the information in the evidence as *presumed* fact(s).

Try to find quality information about your ancestors from the best independent sources available.

Return to Step 1 on page 4, or Step 5 on page 26

HOW TO PLAN FOR A RESEARCH TRIP OR HIRE A PROFESSIONAL RESEARCHER

To discover information about your ancestors may sometimes require you to travel to a place where your ancestor's records are stored. A research trip can be a wonderful experience with great rewards, if you plan well in advance. On other occasions, a professional researcher may be the best resource to help solve a difficult research problem or search hard to get records. Your chances of success in either choice will increase when you follow the suggestions in this section.

Plan a Research Trip

Do Your Homework First, Before You Plan A Trip

Once you have chosen an ancestor or family to learn more about, be sure that you:

1. Clearly define the questions that you want to answer about the ancestor or family. Use the Research Questions form and start a Research Log for each ancestor or family.
2. Visit or correspond with relatives. Gather and search your family records to learn as much as you can about the ancestor or family.
3. Consider a visit to a local Family History Center to see if the type of information you want to answer is there or can be ordered from the Family History Library, in Salt Lake City, Utah. This may save you the expense of an unnecessary trip.

Clearly Define the Purpose of Your Trip

Take a moment to write down what you want to accomplish or produce as a result of your research trip. This will help you plan where you want to go and stay focused when you get there.

Prepare For Each Place

1. Select the places (libraries, archives, courthouses, churches, cemeteries, etc.) that may contain the information you want.
2. Contact each place. Find the address and telephone number at a local library or on the Internet:
   * Learn about the days and hours open and closed, and local holidays or festivals during the time of your visit.
   * Ask if:
     - Fees are required to gain entrance to the place.
     - Special rules or conditions exist to use the records or facilities.
     - An appointment is needed to reserve a study space or a microfilm/fiche reading machine.
     - Interlibrary loans are available.
     - Learn about the type of records available to search in the record collection. Check with a local library for information. Find out if there is a catalog available on the Internet to search.

Plan Your Research Strategy

1. Plan to take the tour. If you are visiting a research facility and an orientation tour is available, learn all that you can about the records and their location before you begin your research.
2. Do the most important searches first. Plan to search all sources that can only be found in the place where you will be. Also, search sources that will require you to look through many rolls of unindexed microfilm.
3. Plan your daily goals. Decide who and what you are going to research.

Research Trip Checklist

When you visit an archive, library, court house, genealogical society, etc. consider these items:

Repository information

* Address
* Directions to facility
* Hours and days open
* Contact person
* Restrictions on briefcases, photocopies, computers, etc.
* Access to records on and off site

Equipment:

- [ ] Calculator
- [ ] Camera and film
- [ ] Computer, laptop
- [ ] Magnifying glass
- [ ] Tape recorder
- [ ] Yellow transparency sheet (use to read faint images on microfilm view area)

Stationery Supplies

- [ ] Envelopes
- [ ] Eraser
- [ ] File folders
- [ ] Glue stick
- [ ] Notebook
- [ ] Notepads
- [ ] Post-it notes
- [ ] Paper clips
- [ ] Paper punch
- [ ] Pencils
- [ ] Pencil sharpener
- [ ] Pens
- [ ] Postage stamps
- [ ] Protractor
- [ ] Ruler or tape measure
- [ ] Scissors
- [ ] Stapler
- [ ] Staple remover
- [ ] Tape

Record Copies (leave originals at home):

- [ ] Pedigree Charts and Family Group Records for the families you are researching.
- [ ] Best possible photocopy of key documents related to your research.

Miscellaneous

- [ ] First Aid kit (include medications)
- [ ] Flashlight (for records tucked away in poorly lighted places.)
- [ ] Identification Card with photo
- [ ] Maps of town, county, state, or region
- [ ] Money (rolls of dimes or quarters) for copy machines and parking meters

Hire a Professional Researcher

Understand the Challenge, Services, Tasks and Fees of a Professional Researcher

1. *The Challenge:* Each genealogical research problem is unique. One research problem can lead to records that are well indexed and easy to use. Another problem can lead to records that are missing or take long periods of time to search. For example, a very common surname such as Smith, Miller, or Brown will require more time to identify because of the number of possible connections to verify. Records in large populated cities can be very time consuming to search, especially if they are unindexed. These types of conditions affect the amount of information a researcher can find in a specified amount of time.

2. *Services*

Professional researchers:
- Trace family lines back in time.
- Identify descendants of a particular individual.
- Find missing relatives and friends.
- Consult about research problems
- Decipher old handwritten records
- Translate foreign records

3. *Tasks*

Researchers perform these tasks:
- Consult with you about your information needs.
- Analyze your records and make research recommendations.
- Conduct research (that may include travel to ancestral cities and record repositories)
- Prepare and respond to correspondence
- Write reports

4. *Fees*
- Professional researchers bill for service time and expenses.
- Service fees vary from $10 to $100 per hour. The U.S. average is $20 to $40 per hour. Some researchers charge a day rate of $125 to $300 per day.
- Expense fees can include: costs to purchase certificates, photocopy information, long distance phone call, postage, forms and supplies, clerical help, travel expenses, etc.

Decide What You Want the Researcher To Do

What service do you need? Do you need one or more family lines traced back two or three generations, regardless of the cost?

Or, will the amount of money you have to hire someone limit their activity to search one record in a distant library or archive?

Do you need to consult with a researcher to get suggestions on how to research a difficult problem? Be very clear about your information needs and any deadlines to receive a final report.

Find a qualified researcher

The chart below shows the names and addresses of three organizations who you can contact and who maintain lists of qualified professional researchers. The individuals on the list may provide research services in a specific record type, country or geographic area, ethnic group, or time period. You can also contact a local genealogical society for help to find a qualified researcher.

Organization and Address	Association of Professional Genealogists P.O. Box 40393, Denver, CO 80204-0393	Board for Certification of Genealogists P.O. Box 14291 Washington, DC 20044	Family History Library 35 North West Temple Street Salt Lake City, UT 84150
Website	<www.apgen.org/directory.html>	<www.bcgcertification.org/rost_ix.html>	None
List Cost	$8 (US), $9 (Canadian), $10 (other countries)	$15.00. Also available at many libraries and archives	List provided at no charge. Send self addressed, stamped envelope.
Qualifications	Members must agree to a code of professional service.	All certified individuals must agree to a "code of ethics."	All accredited individuals must agree to a "code of ethics."
Test	None	Renewal exam every 5 years	Renewal exam every 5 years

Contact Possible Researchers To Do The Work

Call several people who appear to have knowledge about your specific information needs.
- Explain your information needs and what you have in mind for the researcher to do.
- Explain briefly the information you have and what research you have done.
- Find out if he or she is interested and available to work on your project.
- Discuss the strategies he or she might use to search for the information you need and determine how close he or she is to the place where the information may be stored.
- Discuss his or her experience with the type of service you need. If the information you need is in a foreign language, ask about his or her language reading and writing skills.
- Discuss his or her service and expense rates and process to bill you.
- Ask him or her what you can expect to receive at the end of the project (for example, a written report that includes research logs, copies of all research documents, pedigree charts and family group records, and suggestions for future research).
- Ask for the names and phone numbers of one or two persons to contact who he or she has done research for.

Choose a Researcher and Make An Agreement

Decide on a researcher and make a verbal or written agreement about the project.

Provide the Researcher with Information and Fees to Start
- Give the researcher the best photocopies of all charts, forms, documents and other relevant materials. Never give him or her original documents or materials.
- Send whatever fees are required to start the project.
- Follow up often on the progress of the project. If problems occur, try to work through them together. If you are unable to resolve the problems, contact the organization that gave them credentials.

Return to Step 3D on page 20

HOW TO PLAN FOR A RESEARCH TRIP OR HIRE A PROFESSIONAL RESEARCHER

PLACES WHERE RECORDS ARE STORED

TABLE OF CONTENTS

FAMILY HISTORY LIBRARY

35 N. West Temple Street
Salt Lake City, UT, 84150-3400, USA
Phone: 801-240-2331

FAMILY HISTORY CENTERS

There are over 3500 branches of the Family History Library throughout the world. Most centers are located in meetinghouses owned and operated, free to the public, by The Church of Jesus Christ of Latter-day Saints. To find a Family History Center, do one of the following:

1. Locate the name of a city in the state or country of your choice on the list below.
2. Call Family History Center support (toll free at 1-800-346-6044), from 8:00 A.M. to 5:00 P.M. Mountain Time in the United States, Monday - Saturday.
3. Look in your local telephone book under The Church of Jesus Christ of Latter-day Saints.
4. Go to the Internet website:
   <www.familysearch.org/Browse/BrowseLibrary.asp>

NOTE: Before you visit, contact the center to determine the hours of operation and any needed directions to find the center.

U.S. FAMILY HISTORY CENTERS

Under each state are the names of cities or meetinghouses and phone numbers.

ALABAMA

Anniston	256-820-5828
Athens	256-232-1873
Atmore	334-368-4443
Bessemer	205-424-0196
Birmingham	205-967-7279
Cullman	256-739-0891
Decatur	256-350-6586
Dothan	334-793-7425
Enterprise	334-347-3631
Eufaula	334-687-6146
Florence	256-766-5553
Gadsden	256-546-0746
Grove Hill	334-275-3009
Guntersville	256-582-6861
Huntsville	256-721-0905
Indian Springs	256-988-5282
Madison-Harvest	256-722-9450
Mobile	334-344-9270
Monroe	334-862-2423
Montgomery	334-269-9041
Opelika	334-745-2140
Robertsdale	334-947-7400
Scottsboro	256-259-1501
Toxey	205-673-2626
Tuscaloosa	256-758-4820
Wetumpka	334-567-8339

ALASKA

Anchorage	907-277-8433
Bethel	907-543-2007
Cordova	907-424-7771
Delta Junction	907-895-4700
Eagle River	907-694-8538
Fairbanks	907-456-1095
Glennallen	907-822-3328
Haines	907-766-2379
Homer	907-235-7281
Juneau	907-780-4281
Ketchikan	907-225-3291
Kodiak	907-486-3162
Nome	907-985-5729
North Slope	907-852-3291
Palmer	907-745-8003
Sitka	907-747-8991
Soldotna	907-262-4253
Valdez	907-835-4957
Wasilla	907-376-9774
Wrangell	907-874-3778
Yakutat	907-784-3333

ARIZONA

Bagdad	520-633-2073
Buckeye	602-386-4188
Camp Verde	520-649-0116
Casa Grande	520-836-7519
Chandler West	480-857-8640
Chinle	520-871-4605
Chino Valley / Del Rio	520-636-4498
Clifton	520-865-3878
Douglas	520-364-8075
Duncan	520-359-2341
Eagar	520-333-4100
Elfrida	520-642-3482
Glendale	602-973-3216
Globe	520-425-9570
Holbrook	520-524-6663
Kingman	602-753-1316
Lake Havasu City	520-855-8583
Mesa	480-964-1200
Mesa Salt River	480-924-8958
Nogales	520-281-0368
Page	520-645-2328
Paradise Valley	602-953-8160
Parker	520-669-2700
Payson	520-474-3788
Peoria	602-974-2749
Phoenix	602-271-7015
Phoenix 27th Ward	602-243-9413
Phoenix Deer Valley	602-843-6114
Phoenix East	602-266-0128
Phoenix North	602-371-0649
Phoenix West	602-265-7762
Polacca	520-737-2505
Prescott	520-778-2311
Quartzsite	520-927-6080
Safford-Thatcher	520-428-7927
Sahuarita	520-625-4104
San Manuel 1st	520-385-4855
Scottsdale	602-947-3995
Show Low	520-537-2331
Sierra Vista	520-459-1284
Snowflake	520-536-7430
Spring Valley	520-632-7119
St David	520-586-2301
St Johns	520-337-2543
Sunsites	520-826-3455
Tucson	520-298-0905
Tucson North	520-742-3471
Wickenburg	520-684-2446
Willcox	520-384-2751
Winslow	520-289-5496
Woodruff	520-524-2798
Yuma	520-782-6364

ARKANSAS

Blytheville	870-763-2657
Clarksville	501-754-8881
Conway	501-327-1200
El Dorado	870-863-7463
Fort Smith	501-484-5373
Harrison	870-741-8040
Hot Springs	501-262-5640
Jacksonville	501-985-2501
Jones Center Springdale	501-751-8090
Jonesboro	870-935-3400
Little Rock	501-455-4998
Magnolia	870-234-7609
Monticello	870-367-5817
Mountain Home	870-425-7744
N Little Rock Mtn View	870-269-4139
Pocahontas	870-892-4187
Quitman	501-589-3628
Rogers	501-636-0740
Russellville	501-968-3114

CALIFORNIA

Agua Dulce	805-538-1644
Alturas	530-233-2782
Anaheim	714-533-2772
Anderson	530-365-8448
Antioch	925-634-9004
Atascadero	805-466-6103
Auberry	209-855-8863
Auburn	530-823-3139
Bakersfield South	805-831-2036
Bakersfield	805-322-1976
Bakersfield East	805-872-5683
Barstow	760-252-4117
Big Bear	909-585-3801
Bishop	760-873-4881
Blythe	760-922-7641
Burbank	818-843-5024
Camarillo	805-388-7215
Camptonville	530-288-1420
Canoga Park	818-348-8180
Carlsbad	760-434-4941
Carson	310-835-6733
Cedarville	530-279-6347
Cerritos	562-924-3676
Chico	530-343-6641
Chino	909-393-1936
Cloverdale	707-894-9238
Coalinga	209-935-5221
Concord	925-686-1766
Corning	530-824-4445
Corona	909-735-2619
Covina	626-331-7117
Crescent City	707-464-4320
Cypress	714-821-5382
Danville	925-552-5920
Davis	530-662-1538
Delano	805-725-8031
Dixon	707-678-3455
El Cajon	619-588-1426
El Centro	760-352-4686
El Dorado	530-621-1378
Elk Grove	916-688-5554
Escondido	760-745-1662
Etna	530-467-3341
Eureka 1st Ward	707-443-7411
Fairfield	707-425-2027
Fall River	530-336-6965
Fillmore	805-524-1536
Fontana	909-829-6761
Fort Bragg	707-964-5820
Fortuna	707-725-4811
Frazier Park	805-245-1041
Fremont	510-713-1271
Fremont South	510-623-7496
Fresno	559-431-3759
Fresno East	209-291-2448
Fresno North	559-298-876
Fresno West	209-431-4759
Garden Grove	714-554-0592
Glendale	818-241-8763
Glendora	626-335-0923
Golden Gate	415-771-3655
Granada Hills	818-886-5953
Gridley	530-846-3921
Hacienda Heights	626-961-8765
Hanford	559-582-8960
Hayward	510-537-7144
Hemet	909-658-8104
Hesperia	760-868-0883
Highland	909-864-4661
Highlands	707-994-4929
Hollistern	408-637-4917
Huntington Beach North	714-840-1963
Huntington Beach	714-536-4736
Huntington Park West	213-585-7767
Idyllwild	909-659-4679
Jurupa	909-360-8547
Kern Valley	760-379-1658
La Crescenta	818-957-0925
Laguna Niguel	714-580-1908
Lake Elsinore	909-245-4063
Lake Los Angeles	805-264-2557
Lakeport	707-263-1626
Lancaster	805-943-1670
Lancaster East	805-946-4675
Livermore	925-447-2084
Lodi	209-267-1139
Lodi Third Ward	209-369-4148
Livermore	925-447-2084
Loma Rica	530-743-9329
Lompoc	805-735-4939
Long Beach	562-988-0509
Long Beach East	714-821-6914
Loomis	916-652-9970
Los Altos	650-968-1019
Los Angeles	310-474-2202
Los Angeles East	323-726-8145
Los Banos	209-239-5516
Mariposa	209-742-5010
Menifee	909-672-0162
Menlo Park	650-325-9711
Merced	209-722-1307
Milpitas	408-259-5501
Miranda	707-943-3071
Mission Viejo	949-364-2742
Modesto	209-571-0370
Modesto North	209-545-4814
Monterey	831-394-1124
Moreno Valley	909-247-8839
Mount Shasta	530-926-6671
Murrieta	909-698-4983
Napa	707-257-2887
Needles	760-326-3363
Nevada City	530-265-5892
Newbury Park	760-769-4345
Oakhurst	209-683-2930
Oakland	510-531-3905
Ojai	805-640-8164
Orange	714-997-7710
Oroville	530-533-2734
Palm Springs	760-321-0974
Palmdale	661-947-1694

When you have found a center near you, return to Step 3e on page 22.

Palos Verdes	310-541-5644
Pasadena	626-351-8517
Penasquitos	619-484-1729
Pleasanton	925-846-0149
Porterville	559-784-2311
Portola	530-832-4941
Poway	619-487-2304
Quincy	530-283-5175
Rancho Cucamonga	909-899-2337
Red Bluff	530-527-9810
Redding	530-222-4949
Redlands	909-794-3844
Rialto	909-875-2509
Ridgecrest	760-375-6998
Riverside	909-784-1918
Riverside West	909-687-5542
Rocklin	
Sacramento	916-487-2090
San Bernardino	909-881-5355
San Diego Sweetwater	619-472-1506
San Diego	619-584-7668
San Diego East	619-582-0572
San Fernando	818 779-7144
San Francisco	650-873-1928
San Francisco West	650-355-4986
San Jose	408-274-8592
San Luis Obispo	805-543-6328
Santa Barbara	805-682-2092
Santa Clara	408-241-1449
Santa Cruz	408-426-1078
Santa Maria	805-928-4722
Santa Rosa	707-525-0399
Sea Ranch	
Sequoia	559-338-2877
Simi Valley	805-581-2456
Solvang	805-688-3443
Sonoma	707-996-2369
Sonora	209-536-9206
South Lake Tahoe	530-544-1214
Stockton	209-951-7060
Susanville	530-257-4411
Sylmar	818-367-6675
Taft	805-765-6310
Tehachapi	805-822-7909
Thousand Oaks	805-241-9316
Torrance	310-791-6256
Tracy	209-835-1816
Turlock	209-632-9640
Twenty Nine Palms	760-367-0237
Ukiah	707-468-5443
Upland	909-985-8821
Vacaville	707-451-8394
Valencia	805-259-1347
Ventura	805-643-5607
Victorville	760-243-5632
Visalia	559-732-3712
Vista	760-945-6053
Wasco	805-758-2538
Weaverville	530-623-5226
Whittier	562-946-1880
Willits	707-459-5332
Willows	530-934-4883
Yuba City	530-673-0113
Yucca Valley	760-369-7430

COLORADO

Alamosa	719-589-5511
Arvada	303-421-0920
Aurora	303-367-0570
Boulder	303-665-4685
Brighton	303-659-8489
Canon City	719-276-3038
Colorado Springs North	719-531-9621
Colorado Springs	719-634-0572
Colorado Springs East	719-268-9185
Columbine	303-973-3727
Cortez	970-564-1064
Delta	970-874-3444
Denver	303-756-0220
Denver North	303-451-7177
Durango	970-259-1061
Eagle Valley	970-524-9353
Fort Collins	970-226-5999
Fort Morgan	970-867-9523
Glenwood Springs	970-963-2531
Golden	970-668-5633
Grand Junction	970-243-2782
Greeley	970-356-1904
La Junta	719-384-0427
Lakewood	303-935-3003
Littleton	303-798-6461
Longmont	303-772-4373
Loveland	970-667-1542
Manassa	719-274-4032

Meeker	970-824-2763
Montrose	970-249-4739
Naturita	970-865-2317
Pagosa Springs Branch	970-731-2623
Paonia	970-527-4084
Pueblo	719-564-0793
Rangely	970-675-8678
Rifle	970-625-1883
Salida Pueblo	719-539-4987
Steamboat Springs	970-879-0224
Sterling	970-522-6407

CONNECTICUT

Goshen	860-491-5227
Groton	860-536-5102
Hartford	860-242-1607
Madison	203-245-8267
Manchester	860-643-4003
New Canaan	203-966-8475
New Haven	203-387-2012
Newtown	203-426-1752
Southington	860-628-0617

DELAWARE

Dover	302-697-2700
Newark	302-456-9301
Wilmington	302-654-1911

FLORIDA

Apalachicola	850-670-8501
Arcadia	941-993-0996
Belle Glade	561-996-6355
Bonifay	850-547-4557
Bradenton	941-755-6906
Brooksville	352-796-7403
Bunnell	904-437-7881
Clermont	352-242-6363
Cocoa	407-636-2431
Daytona Beach	904-257-9223
Defuniak Springs	850-892-3167
Deland	904-736-1800
Fort Myers	941-275-0001
Fort Pierce	561-464-0600
Fort Walton Beach	850-244-3338
Gibsonia	941-853-1582
Hialeah Gardens	305-828-3460
Homestead	305-246-4194
Jacksonville East	904-743-0527
Jacksonville West	904-272-1150
Key West	305-294-9400
Lake Butler	904-496-2245
Lake City	904-755-9432
Lake Mary	407-333-0137
Lakeland	941-665-6730
Lecanto	352-746-5943
Leesburg	352-787-3990
Liberty	904-643-5600
Live Oak	904-362-3573
MacClenny	904-259-6910
Marathon	305-743-9016
Marianna	850-482-8159
Mexico Beach	850-648-8182
Miami	305-485-8174
Miami Shores	305-899-8606
Naples	941-455-3544
Navarre	850-939-4636
Newport Richey	727-868-8225
Ocala	352-351-4163
Orlando	407-895-4832
Orlando South	407-826-8970
Palm Beach	561-533-8803
Palm Beach Gardens	561-626-7989
Panama City	850-785-9290
Pensacola	850-969-1254
Plantation	954-472-0524
Pompano Beach	561-395-6644
Port Charlotte	941-627-6446
Sarasota	941-922-2550
St Augustine	904-797-9412
St Petersburg	727-399-8018
Starke	904-964-8145
Stuart	561-287-0167
Tallahasse	850-222-8870
Tampa	813-971-2869
Vero Beach	561-569-5122
Wauchula	941-773-3532
Winter Haven	941-299-1691

GEORGIA

Albany	912-888-7588
Athens	706-543-3052
Atlanta	404-755-7624
Augusta	706-860-1024

Cochran	912-934-7212
Columbus	706-563-7216
Conyers	770-760-7941
Dahlonega	706-265-2314
Douglas	912-384-0607
Douglasville	770-949-5168
Jesup	912-427-4469
Jonesboro	770-477-5985
Kingsland	912-265-5912
Kingsland Ward	912-729-5696
La Grange	706-882-2201
Lawrenceville	770-962-5650
Macon	912-788-5885
Marietta East	770-973-4510
Milledgeville	912-454-4090
Moultrie	912-985-5671
Newnan	770-254-9857
Perry	912-987-0030
Powder Springs	770-943-9393
Rome	706-235-2281
Roswell	770-594-1706
Savannah	912-927-6543
Sugar Hill	770-536-4391
Sugar Hill Ward	770-271-3450
Swainsboro	912-237-2645
Tifton	912-382-2606
Tucker	770-723-9941
Valdosta	912-242-2300
Waycross	912-283-2661

HAWAII

Hilo	808-935-0711
Honokaa	808-775-7348
Honolulu	808-955-8910
Honolulu West	808-845-9701
Honomakau	808-889-5473
Johnston Island	808-621-3044
Ka'u	808-929-7123
Kahului	808-877-8841
Kaneohe	808-247-3134
Kauai	808-246-9119
Keei	808-328-8171
Kona	808-329-4469
Laie	808-293-2133
Makakilo	808-678-0752
Mililani	808-623-1712
Molokai	808-553-5296
Waimea	808-885-4684
Waipahu	808-678-0752

IDAHO

American Falls	208-226-9610
Arimo	208-254-3846
Ashton	208-652-7548
Bancroft	208-648-7337
Bear Lake	208-847-0340
Blackfoot	208-785-5022
Blackfoot West	208-684-3784
Boise	208-338-3811
Bonners Ferry	208-267-3802
Burley	208-678-7286
Caldwell	208-454-8324
Carey	208-788-9810
Cascade	208-382-3230
Coeur D'Alene	208-765-0150
Driggs	208-354-2253
Eagle	208-939-4738
Emmett	208-365-6142
Firth	208-346-6011
Fruitland	208-452-4345
Garden Valley	208-462-3036
Glenns Ferry	208-366-2027
Grace	208-425-3121
Grand View	208-834-2717
Grangeville	208-983-2110
Idaho Falls South	208-524-1991
Idaho Falls	208-524-5291
Idaho Falls Ammon	208-529-4087
Idaho Falls East	208-524-1038
State Correctional Facility	208-424-3732
Kamiah	208-935-0831
Kellogg	208-682-2911
Kuna	208-922-5822
Lewiston	208-746-6910
Malad	208-766-2332
McCall	208-634-5910
McCammon	208-254-3259
Meridian East	208-376-0452
Meridian South	208-362-2638
Meridian West	208-288-1338
Moore	208-554-2806
Mountain Home	208-587-5249
Nampa	208-467-5827
Orofino	208-476-3914

Pocatello	208-232-9262
Preston South	208-852-0710
Priest River	208-437-2474
Rexburg	208-356-2386
Rigby	208-745-8660
Rigby East	208-745-7042
Roberts	208-663-4389
Salmon	208-756-2371
Sandpoint	208-263-8721
Shelley	208-357-3128
Soda Springs	208-547-3232
St Anthony	208-624-4396
St Maries	208-245-2224
Twin Falls	208-733-8073
Weiser	208-549-1575

ILLINOIS

Alton	618-466-4352
Bourbonnais	815-939-2528
Buffalo Grove	847-913-5387
Carbondale	618-549-3034
Centralia	618-532-3484
Champaign	217-352-8063
Chicago Heights	708-756-1280
Crystal Lake	815-459-7475
Danville	217-446-5887
Decatur 1st & 2nd	217-875-9396
Eldorado	618-273-8172
Foxcroft	618-937-4755
Hyde Park	773-493-1830
Jacksonville	217-245-8113
Joliet	815-725-8621
Keosauqua	319-293-3455
Litchfield	217-324-2396
Macomb	309-836-3201
Mattoon	217-234-3362
Morris	815-941-4133
Naperville	630-505-0233
Nauvoo	217-453-6347
Newell K. Whitney Home	217-453-2733
O'Fallon	618-632-0210
Orlan Park	708-361-5474
Ottawa	815-434-1197
Peoria	309-682-4073
Quincy	217-224-3220
Rockford	815-399-2660
Schaumburg	847-885-4130
Springfield	217-585-1294
Sterling	815-625-1229
Westchester	709-562-8679
Wilmette Ilinois	847-251-9818

INDIANA

Anderson	765-644-6417
Batesville	812-934-3443
Bedford	812-275-6672
Bloomington	812-333-0050
Brownsburg	317-852-2559
Columbus	812-376-7073
Crawfordsville	765-362-8006
Evansville	812-471-0191
Fishers	317-842-6180
Fort Wayne	219-485-9581
Griffith	219-838-8189
Hebron	219-996-6119
Huntington	219-356-7171
Indianapolis	317-888-6002
Kokomo	765-453-0092
Lafayette	765-463-5079
Marion	765-662-3311
Muncie	765-288-9139
New Albany	812-949-7532
Peru	765-473-4933
Richmond	765-966-2366
South Bend	219-243-1633
Terre Haute	812-234-0269
Valparaiso	219-464-4411
Vincennes	812-882-4022
Warsaw	219-267-2118

IOWA

Ames	515-232-3634
Atlantic	712-243-2507
Burlington	319-754-7974
Cedar Falls/Waterloo	319-338-5306
Cedar Rapids	319-363-7178
Davenport	319-386-7547
Des Moines	515-225-0416
Dubuque	319-583-6851
Fairfield	515-472-9513
Fort Dodge	515-576-6180
Glenwood	712-527-9627
Iowa City	319-338-5306
Marshalltown	515-752-3284
Mason City	515-424-4211
Mount Vernon	319-895-6468

Muscatine	319-263-5612
Newton	515-792-2784
Osceola	515-342-6333
Ottumwa	515-682-1622
Sheldon	712-342-9932
Shenandoah	712-246-4491
Sioux City	712-255-9686
Spencer	712-262-6172
Storm Lake	712-732-4527

KANSAS

Burlington	316-364-8077
Colby	785-572-6605
Concordia	785-243-5072
Emporia	316-343-1304
Great Bend	316-793-7328
Hays	785-625-2817
Hutchinson	316-665-1187
Independence	316-331-7323
Iola	316-365-2777
Junction City	785-762-8662
Kansas City 2nd	913-299-2876
Kansas West District	316-225-6540
Lawrence	785-843-4460
Leavenworth	913-651-8551
Lenexa	913-722-0230
Liberal	316-624-3544
Manhattan	785-539-5445
Olathe	913-829-1775
Ottawa	785-242-5611
Paola	913-294-4411
Phillipsburg	913-543-5851
Salina	785-827-0058
Topeka	785-271-6818
Wichita	316-683-2951

KENTUCKY

Ashland	606-836-1272
Beattyville	606-464-3378
Bowling Green	502-842-7148
Brandenburg	502-422-2533
Corbin	606-528-2898
Elizabethtown	270-737-5037
Fulton	502-472-3634
Glasgow Branch	502-651-5858
Hopkinsville	502-886-1616
Lexington	606-269-2722
Louisville	502-426-8174
Madisonville	502-825-1070
Martin	606-285-3133
Morgantown	270-728-3491
Northern Wards	606-331-7615
Owensboro	502-685-3396
Owingsville	606-674-6626
Paducah	270-443-8947
Tompkinsville	270-487-0620

LOUISIANA

Alexandria	318-448-1842
Baker	225-775-0383
Baton Rouge	225-769-8913
Denham Springs	225-664-8979
Gonzales	225-644-0581
Lafayette	318-984-7182
Monroe	318-322-7009
New Orleans	504-885-3936
Opelousas	318-942-8081
Ruston	318-255-8379
Shreveport	318-868-5169
Slidell	504-641-3982
Thibodaux	504-876-0221
Winnfield	318-628-6945

MAINE

Augusta	207-582-1827
Bangor	207-947-5624
Caribou	207-492-4381
Farmington	207-778-4038
Oxford	207-743-8125
Portland	207-892-2098
Rockland-Bangor	207-594-1018
Topsham	207-725-8427
Waterville	207-873-0054

MARYLAND

Annapolis	410-757-4173
Baltimore	410-686-6709
Columbia	410-465-1642
Cumberland	301-724-1609
Frederick	301-698-0406
Hampstead	410-239-2461
Hancock	301-678-6007

Lexington Park	301-863-8002
Salisbury	410-742-8568
Seneca	301-972-5897
Suitland	301-423-8294
Washington D.C.	301-587-0042

MASSACHUSETTS

Amherst	413-549-5053
Belmont	617-489-4125
Boston	781-235-2164
Brewster	508-896-9863
Cambridge	617-491-4749
Hingham	508-543-0298
Hingham Ward	781-749-9835
Lynnfield	781-334-5586
Martha's Vineyard	508-693-8642
North Dartmouth	508-994-8215
Worcester	508-852-7000

MINNESOTA

Anoka	612-425-1865
Austin	507-433-9042
Bemidji	218-751-9129
Brainerd	218-828-4701
Burnsville	612-835-0053
Detroit Lakes	218-847-3260
Duluth	218-726-1361
Faribault	507-334-7046
Mankato	507-625-8342
Marshall	507-532-4913
Minneapolis	612-544-2479
Pipestone	507-825-2993
Princeton	612-389-1289
Rochester	507-281-6641
St Cloud	320-252-4355
St Paul	651-770-3213
Virginia	218-749-2490

MISSISSIPPI

Booneville	601-728-9011
Columbus	601-328-2788
Greenville	601-332-8176
Gulfport	228-832-0195
Hattiesburg	601-268-3733
Jackson	601-924-2686
Liberty	601-657-8903
Meridian	601-483-7426
Natchez	601-442-1893
Oxford	601-234-7586
Philadelphia	601-656-8801
Raytown	601-859-3591
Red Star	601-833-6693
Senatobia	662-562-7161
Tupelo	601-844-2092

MISSOURI

Adam-ondi-Ahman	660-828-4325
Aurora	417-678-4399
Ava	417-683-4525
Bolivar	417-777-5969
Branson	417-335-6833
Cameron	816-632-3770
Cape Girardeau	573-334-7644
Clinton	660-885-6839
Columbia	573-443-2048
Excelsior Springs	816-637-8383
Farmington	573-756-6521
Fulton	573-642-6814
Hannibal	573-221-5147
Independence	816-461-0245
Jefferson City	573-893-3847
Joplin	417-623-6506
Kansas City	816-941-7389
Kansas City (Blue Springs)	816-228-3835
Kirksville	660-665-1549
Lebanon	417-588-2928
Liberty	816-781-8295
Maryville	660-582-8536
Moberly	660-263-5829
Monett	417-235-5147
Nevada	417-667-2781
Osage Beach	573-348-3424
Poplar Bluff	573-785-0211
Rolla	573-364-1451
Sedalia	660-827-6720
Springfield	417-887-8229
St Charles	314-272-5002
St Joseph	816-232-2428
St Louis	314-993-2328
St Louis North	314-731-5373
St Louis South	314-789-4323

When you have found a center near you, return to Step 3e on page 22.

Stockton	417-276-4125	Pahrump	775-727-5229	Owego	607-797-3900
Tipton	660-433-5872	Panaca	702-728-4699	Owego	607-687-5137
Trenton	660-359-3352	Reno	775-826-1130	Plainview	516-433-0122
Washington	314-239-7718	Smokey Valley	702-377-2060	Plattsburg	518-561-1092
West Plains	417-256-1431	Tonopah	702-482-5492	Potsdam	315-265-6228
Willard	417-742-3841	Wells	775-752-3763	Poughkeepsie	914-462-2470
		Winnemucca	702-623-4448	Pulaski	315-298-4422
MONTANA		Yerington	702-463-3600	Queens East	718-478-5337
				Rochester	716-271-5040
Belt	406-277-4442	**NEW HAMPSHIRE**		Rochester Palmyra	716-248-9930
Billings	406-656-5559			Schoharie Valley	518-868-2049
Billings East	406-259-3348	Concord	603-225-2848	Syracuse	315-457-5172
Bozeman	406-586-3880	Exeter	603-778-2509	Utica	315-736-7414
Butte	406-494-2413	Lebanon	603-448-4374	Watertown	315-788-4161
Chester	406-759-5390	Nashua	603-594-8888	Wellsville	716-593-3481
Choteau	406-466-2725	Randolph	603-466-3417	Westchester	914-723-4022
Colstrip	406-748-2039			Yorktown	914-941-9754
Conrad	406-278-5484	**NEW JERSEY**			
Cut Bank	406-873-2806	Caldwell	973-226-8975	**NORTH CAROLINA**	
Darby	406-821-3220	Cherry Hill	856-795-8841		
Dillon	406-683-2033	Clinton	908-713-0292	Albemarle	704-982-2018
Eureka	406-296-3461	East Brunswick	732-254-1480	Asheville	828-684-6646
Fort Benton	406-622-3662	Eatontown	732-542-2691	Boone	704-262-1376
Glasgow	406-228-2382	Emerson	201-262-7357	Caswell	336-421-0394
Glendive	406-365-2124	Fardale	201-327-1940	Charlotte South	704-541-1451
Great Falls	406-453-1625	Ledgewood	973-347-6833	Charlotte	704-509-6407
Great Falls East	406-454-1611	Morristown	973-539-5362	Cherokee	704-497-7651
Havre	406-265-7982	Princeton	609-452-0802	Durham	919-967-0988
Helena	406-443-0716	Scotch Plains	908-889-0628	Eden	336-623-1797
Jordan	406-557-2307	Short Hills	973-379-7315	Elizabeth City	252-335-7892
Kalispell	406-752-5446	Toms River	732-349-5947	Fayetteville	910-860-1350
Lewistown	406-538-9058	Union City	201-866-8118	Forest City	828-245-8561
Libby	406-293-4757	Vineland	609-696-5002	Franklin	704-369-8329
Livingston	406-222-3570			Gastonia	704-865-6704
Malta	406-654-1207	**NEW MEXICO**		Goldsboro	919-731-2130
Miles City	406-232-1487	Alamogordo	505-437-8772	Greensboro	336-288-6539
Missoula	406-543-6148	Albuquerque	505-343-0456	Greenville	252-756-5890
Polson	406-883-2565	Albuquerque East	505-293-5610	Harkers Island	252-728-2260
Seeley Lake	406-677-2575	Albuquerque South	505-266-4867	Hickory	828-324-2823
Sheridan	406-842-5860	Animas	505-548-2318	Kannapolis	704-932-4426
Sidney	406-482-3250	Carlsbad	505-885-1368	Kinston	252-522-2116
Stevensville	406-777-5018	Clovis	505-769-1350	Lake Norman	704-664-7127
Superior	406-822-4758	Deming	505-544-0286	Lumberton	910-738-3461
Thompson Falls	406-827-9757	Edgewood	505-281-5384	Marion	828-652-2820
Three Forks	406-285-3755	Espanola	505-753-3751	Morganton	828-433-5734
Townsend	406-266-4255	Farmington	505-325-5813	Murphy	828-837-8509
Yellowstone North	406-848-7509	Grants	505-287-2470	Nags Head	252-441-5925
		Hobbs	505-392-6200	New Bern	252-638-8410
NEBRASKA		Las Cruces	505-382-0618	North Wilkesboro	336-667-2832
Alliance	308-762-1308	Los Alamos	505-662-3186	Pinehurst	910-692-8085
Beatrice	402-223-2581	Los Lunas	505-865-0788	Raleigh	919-783-7752
Blair	402-426-3299	Luna	505-547-2762	Roanoke Rapids	252-535-2989
Chadron	308-432-5657	Ramah	505-783-4536	Rocky Mount	252-937-4086
Columbus	402-564-6896	Raton	505-445-9226	Statesville	704-872-6693
Gordon	308-282-0635	Roswell	505-624-1761	Wilmington	910-395-4456
Grand Island	308-382-9418	Ruidoso	505-336-4359	Winston-Salem	336-768-8878
Hastings	402-463-3402	Santa Fe	505-986-8254		
Kearney Ward	308-234-3417	Silver City	505-388-1068	**NORTH DAKOTA**	
Lincoln	402-423-4561	Socorro	505-835-4806	Bismarck	701-223-6384
Macy	402-837-5204	Taos	505-750-2018	Dickinson	701-264-7354
McCook	308-345-5406	Tres Piedras	505-751-0994	Fargo	701-232-4003
Norfolk	402-371-7441	Tucumcari	505-461-9676	Grand Forks	701-746-6126
North Platte	308-532-0940	White Rock	505-672-9888	Minot	701-838-4486
O'Neill	402-336-2167			Wahpeton	701-642-2463
Omaha	402-393-7641	**NEW YORK**		Williston	701-572-3502
Papillion	402-339-0461	Albany	518-463-4581		
Scottsbluff	308-635-7012	Auburn	315-253-0670	**OHIO**	
Sidney	308-254-4025	Brockport	716-637-2030	Adams	937-695-0030
		Bronx	718-561-7824	Akron	330-630-3365
NEVADA		Brooklyn	718-434-8245	Ashtabula	440-993-3616
Alamo-Hiko	775-725-3411	Buffalo	716-688-2439	Athens	740-797-3898
Austin	702-964-2336	Cortland	607-753-6418	Canton	330-497-2441
Beatty	702-553-2051	Elmira	607-739-8002	Chillicothe	614-774-4533
Black Mountain	702-566-8190	Fayette	315-539-8167	Cincinnati	513-531-5624
Boulder City	702-293-3304	Fredonia	716-673-1718	Cincinnati 5th & 7th	513-753-3464
Carson City	702-884-2064	Gloversville	518-725-4417	Cincinnati North	513-489-3036
Elko East	775-778-9866	Ithaca	607-257-0428	Cleveland	440-777-1518
Elko West	775-738-4565	Jamestown	716-487-0830	Columbus East	614-866-7686
Ely	702-289-2287	Kingston	914-382-2170	Columbus North	614-761-1898
Fallon	702-423-8888	Lake Placid	518-523-2889	Columbus Westland/Scioto	614-875-8680
Fallon South	702-423-9338	Lowville	315-376-9386	Dayton	937-854-4566
Fernley	702-575-4474	Lynbrook	516-599-8079	Dayton East	937-878-9551
Hawthorne	702-945-2847	Medina	716-798-4252	Fairfield/Hamilton	513-844-8866
Las Vegas East	702-641-6219	Middletown	914-692-0364	Findlay	419-422-8668
Las Vegas North	702-382-9695	New York City	212-873-1690	Galion	419-468-2088
Las Vegas Red Rock	702-878-0361	Newburgh	914-564-6785	Georgetown	937-378-3186
Las Vegas Warm Springs	702-361-5102	Norwich	607-336-6341	Kirtland	440-256-8808
Logandale	702-398-3266	Olean	716-372-5515	Lima	419-227-2537
Lovelock	702-273-7380	Oneonta	607-432-8195	Lisbon	330-424-3333
Mesquite	702-346-2342	Orchard Park	716-662-3117	Mansfield	419-756-5530

Marion	614-389-3212
Medina	330-723-5200
Middletown	513-423-9642
Mount Vernon	740-392-7016
Oxford	513-523-0643
Rootstown	330-325-7627
Sandusky	419-626-9860
Toledo	419-872-9491
Warren/Youngstown	330-759-0231
Wauseon	419-337-1880
Westerville	614-899-9968
Wilmington	937-382-1510
Wintersville	740-266-6334
Zanesville	740-454-0108

OKLAHOMA

Ardmore	405-226-2134
Bartlesville	918-333-3135
Claremore	918-342-0101
Cleveland	918-358-3743
Cushing	918-225-3234
Enid	580-234-3313
Lawton	580-536-1303
McAlester	918-423-3762
Muskogee	918-687-8861
Norman	405-364-8337
Oklahoma City	405-721-8455
Oklahoma City South	405-794-3800
Owasso	918-272-2048
Pawhuska	918-287-2107
Ponca City	580-765-3464
Sapulpa	918-224-7585
Seminole	405-382-5111
Shawnee	405-273-7943
Stillwater	405-377-4122
Tulsa	918-747-3966
Tulsa East	918-437-5690
Woodward	405-256-5113

OREGON

Astoria	503-325-8346
Baker	541-523-2397
Beaverton	503-644-7782
Beaverton West Bend	541-382-9947
Brookings	541-469-5754
Burns	541-573-2120
Cave Junction	541-592-3661
Central Point	541-664-5356
Chiloquin	541-783-2729
Coos Bay	541-756-3575
Corvallis	503-758-1156
Cottage Grove	541-942-2670
Elgin	541-437-4061
Enterprise	541-426-3342
Eugene West	541-343-3741
Florence	541-997-7268
Gold Beach	541-247-6496
Grants Pass	541-476-1926
Gresham	503-665-1524
Gresham South	503-668-4811
Hermiston	541-567-3445
Hillsboro	503-640-4658
John Day	541-575-1817
Klamath Falls	541-884-7998
La Grande	541-963-5003
La Pine	541-536-5636
Lake Oswego	503-638-1410
Lakeview	503-947-2389
Lebanon	541-451-3992
Lincoln City	541-994-2998
McMinnville	503-434-5681
Medford	541-773-3363
Mid-Columbia	541-386-3539
Milwaukie	503-722-8766
Molalla	503-829-5350
Monmouth	503-838-2964
Myrtle Creek	541-863-4337
Newberg	503-538-3510
Newport	541-265-7333
Nyssa	541-372-5255
Oakridge	541-782-3120
Ontario	541-889-7835
Oregon City	503-655-9908
Pendleton	541-276-3117
Portland	503-235-9090
Portland East	503-252-1081
Prineville	541-447-1488
Reedsport	541-271-3736
Roseburg	541-672-1237
Salem	503-378-0383
Salem East	503-371-0453
Seaside	503-738-7543

St Helens	503-397-1300
Sweet Home	541-367-3360
The Dalles	541-298-5815
Tillamook	503-842-2781
Tualatin	503-692-0481
Willamina	503-876-3452
Wilsonville	503-685-7383
Woodburn	583-981-4731

PENNSYLVANIA

Allentown	610-866-3611
Altoona	814-238-4560
Altoona Ward	814-696-0341
Berwick	717-759-1637
Butler	724-482-2129
Carlisle	717-697-8092
Chambersburg	717-263-8679
Doylestown	215-348-0645
Dubois [Kane]	814-837-9729
Dubois Ward	814-583-5837
Erie	814-866-3611
Fairview	717-762-2268
Franklin	814-437-5561
Gettysburg	717-624-9455
Harrisburg	717-295-1719
Indiana	724-349-1337
Johnstown	814-269-4652
Meadville	814-336-5064
Nazareth	610-759-9486
Philadelphia Metro	215-329-3692
Pittsburgh	412-921-2115
Pottstown	610-327-3166
Reading	610-929-0235
Scranton	570-587-5123
Sunbury	570-473-9946
Towanda	717-565-5181
Valley Forge	610-356-8507
Warren	814-726-2455
Washington	724-222-9474
Williamsport	717-494-1699
York	717-846-4539

RHODE ISLAND

Providence	401 463-8150

SOUTH CAROLINA

Aiken	803-648-0726
Beaufort	843-525-1823
Charleston	843-766-6017
Columbia	803-782-7141
Florence	843-662-2967
Gaffney	864-489-2615
Georgetown	843-761-8671
Greenville	864-627-0553
Greenwood	864-223-0937
Myrtle Beach	843-449-1166
Ridgeland	803-726-8421
Seneca	864-882-3147
Spartanburg	864-585-5943
Sumter	803-481-8300

SOUTH DAKOTA

Aberdeen	605-225-0601
Belle Fourche	605-892-3700
Brookings	605-692-9350
Gettysburg	605-765-9270
Hot Springs	605-745-6119
Huron	605-352-6849
Madison	605-256-6335
Pierre	605-224-2586
Rapid City	605-343-8656
Rosebud	605-747-2128
Sioux Falls	605-361-1070
Vermillion	605-624-7139
Yankton	605-665-5307

TENNESSEE

Athens	423-745-0102
Chattanooga	423-892-7632
Clarksville	931-358-9635
Columbia	931-381-3650
Cookeville	913-526-3116
Crossville	931-484-2507
Cumberland Gap	615-869-2481
Fayetteville	931-433-6296
Franklin	615-794-4251
Gallatin	615-452-2741
Grove Park	423-688-7411

Haywood	615-833-8916
Jackson	901-664-2274
Jamestown	615-879-7356
Kingsport	423-245-2321
Knoxville	423-693-8252
Maryville	423-984-6390
McMinnville	931-473-1053
Memphis	901-754-2545
Memphis North	901-388-9974
Murfreesboro	615-893-1349
Nashville	615-859-6926
Oak Ridge	423-483-6401
Paris	901-642-2285
Sevierville	423-453-9541
Smyrna	615-355-9268
Tullahoma	931-455-5230

TEXAS

Abilene	915-673-8836
Alvin	281-585-3033
Amarillo	806-352-2409
Arlington	817-446-7088
Austin	512-837-3626
Austin Oak Hills	512-892-4936
Azle	817-444-6691
Bastrop	512-321-4142
Bay City	409-245-3152
Baytown	281-428-2204
Beaumont	409-727-3548
Beeville	512-358-7313
Big Spring	915-263-4411
Boerne	210-249-9197
Borger	806-274-4685
Brownsville	956-546-6422
Brownwood	915-643-6635
Canyon Lake	210-899-5118
Clear Lake	281-488-4406
Cleburne	817-645-0566
Cleveland	281-592-6364
College Station	409-846-3516
Conroe	409-756-4004
Corpus Christi	361-993-2970
Corsicana	903-872-4760
Cypress	281-251-5931
Dallas	972-709-0066
Dallas East	214-342-2642
Decatur	940-627-5534
Del Rio	830-775-4511
Denton	940-387-3065
Eagle Pass	830-773-2753
El Paso	915-599-8565
El Paso 1st & 3rd	915-565-4323
El Paso 6th/7th	915-757-1215
El Paso Mount Franklin	915-581-8849
Fort Worth	817-292-8393
Fredericksburg	210-997-5018
Friendswood	281-996-9346
Gainesville	817-665-3742
Galveston	409-744-7938
Georgetown	512-863-8221
Gilmer	903-843-5805
Graham	940-549-5512
Granbury	817-573-6825
Greenville	903-455-1614
Harlingen	956-421-2028
Hondo	830-426-4203
Houston	713-785-2105
Houston East	281-991-8479
Houston North	281-893-5381
Houston South	281-240-1524
Hurst	817-284-4472
Katy	281-578-8338
Kerrville	830-895-3335
Killeen	254-526-2918
Kingsville	512-592-3630
Kingwood	281-360-1352
Lake Jackson	409-297-8454
Laredo	956-722-8474
League City	281-538-1283
Lewisville	972-393-6976
Livingston	409-327-5680
Longview	903-297-1349
Lubbock	806-792-5040
Lufkin	409-637-7750
Magnolia	713-521-9728
McAllen	956-682-1061
McKinney	972-547-0019
Midland	915-697-6755

When you have found a center near you, return to Step 3e on page 22.

PLACES WHERE RECORDS ARE STORED

Monahans	915-943-4549	Kearns North	801-964-7363
Odessa	915-337-3112	Laketown	435-946-3262
Old Katy	281-391-7689	Layton Hills	801-774-2070
Orange	409-883-7969	Layton Valley View	801-543-2908
Pampa	806-669-9547	Lehi	801-768-3054
Paris	903-784-0788	Lindon	801-785-7586
Pecos	915-447-6222	Loa	435-836-2322
Pine Trails	281-458-1526	Logan Cache	435-755-7999
Plainview	806-293-5897	Magna Central	801-252-2530
Plano	972-867-6479	Magna East	801-252-2539
Pleasanton	830-569-5703	Manila	435-784-3381
Queen City	903-796-5376	Manti	435-835-8888
Raymondville	956-689-5408	Mapleton	801-489-2999
Richardson	972-680-8654	Midvale Union Fort	801-562-8085
Rockdale	512-446-6371	Milford 1st & 2nd Ward	435-387-2419
Rockwall	972-475-8606	Moab	435-259-5563
San Angelo	915-651-5970	Monroe Stake	435-527-4612
San Antonio	210-673-9404	Monticello	435-587-2139
San Antonio 5th & 10th	210-431-9854	Morgan	801-829-6261
San Antonio East	210-656-4111	Moroni	435-436-8497
San Antonio North	210-736-2940	Mount Timpanogos	801-763-2093
San Marcos	512-353-8672	Murray Little Cottonwood	801-264-4137
Sealy	409-885-6023	Murray South	801-264-4145
Seguin	830-372-5212	Murray West	801-264-4152
Shadowdale	713-466-7706	Nephi	435-623-1378
Silsbee	409-385-9692	Ogden	801-626-1132
Stephenville	254-968-6294	Orem Geneva Heights	801-222-0529
Stone Oak	210-497-7762	Orem Lakeridge	801-222-0497
Sweetwater	915-235-2066	Orem Park	801-222-0399
Texarkana-New Boston	903-831-5225	Orem Sharon Park	801-222-0319
The Colony	972-370-3537	Orem Sunset Heights	801-222-0449
Tyler	903-509-8322	Panguitch	435-676-2201
Uvalde	830-278-1501	Park City	435-649-0725
Victoria	361-575-0055	Parowan	435-477-8077
Waller	409-372-5738	Payson	801-465-1349
Weatherford	817-594-4064	Pleasant Grove Grove Creek	801-785-7570
Weslaco/Mercedes	956-514-2438	Price	435-637-2071
Wharton	409-532-3002	Provo Bonneville	801-370-6674
Wichita Falls	940-696-9811	Provo East	801-370-6713
Wills Point	903-873-4361	Provo Edgemont	801-222-0567
Yorktown Kenedy	512-564-3884	Provo Edgemont North	801-222-3108
		Provo South	801-370-6830
UTAH		Provo Sunset	801-370-6849
Alpine North	801-763-2008	Richfield	435-896-8057
Altamont	435-454-3422	Riverton	801-253-7085
American Fork	801-763-2014	Roosevelt	435-722-9213
Beaver	435-438-5262	Salem	801-423-2329
Bennion	801-964-7201	Salt Lake Big Cottonwood	801-273-3719
Blanding	435-678-2728	Salt Lake Canyon Rim	801-484-4441
Boulder	435-335-7302	Salt Lake Emigration	801-578-6661
Bountiful North Canyon	801-299-4239	Salt Lake Granger South	801-964-7250
Brigham City	435-723-5995	Salt Lake Granger West	801-964-7490
BYU 8th Stake	801-370-6626	Salt Lake Hillside	801-584-3142
Cache	435-755-5594	Salt Lake Holladay South	801-273-3784
Canyon Springs	801-576-2861	Salt Lake Hunter	801-964-3012
Castle Dale	435-381-2899	Salt Lake Hunter West	801-252-2560
Castle Valley	435-259-7028	Salt Lake Jordan North	801-964-7465
Cedar City	435-586-2296	Salt Lake Millcreek	801-264-4052
Cedar City North	435-586-0432	Salt Lake Monument Park	801-584-3163
Circleville	435-577-2528	Salt Lake Mt Olympus	801-273-3815
Coalville	435-336-1478	Salt Lake Olympus	801-273-3836
Cove Point	801-370-6757	Salt Lake Park	801-578-6719
Delta	435-864-3312	Salt Lake Rose Park	801-578-6769
Draper	801-576-2839	Salt Lake Wasatch	801-944-2075
Duchesne	435-738-5371	Salt Lake Winder	801-273-3862
East Carbon	435-888-9989	Sandy Cottonwood Creek	801-944-2140
Enterprise	435-878-2520	Sandy Crescent	801-576-2891
Escalante	435-679-8693	Sandy Crescent Park	801-576-2949
Escalante Ward	435-826-4217	Sandy Crescent South	801-576-2953
Farmington	801-451-1998	Sandy Crescent West	801-576-2971
Ferron	435-384-3288	Sandy East	801-576-2987
Fillmore	435-743-6614	Sandy Granite South	801-944-2131
Genola	801-754-3965	Sandy Hidden Valley	801-567-2834
Glendale	435-648-2306	Santa Clara	435-628-0054
Goshen	801-667-3232	Santaquin	801-754-3881
Grantsville West	435-884-1220	Snow College	435-283-6489
Green River	435-564-3582	South Jordan	801-253-7008
Gunnison	435-528-7347	Spanish Fork	801-798-5535
Gunnison Correctional Facility	435-528-6233	Springville	801-489-2956
Hanksville	435-542-3201	St George	435-673-4591
Heber City	435-654-2760	St George Morningside	435-652-1425
Helper	435-472-3798	Syracuse	801-774-2188
Highland	801-768-1381	Taylorsville West	801-964-3009
Huntington	435-687-9090	Tooele Valley	435-882-7514
Hurricane	435-635-2174	Tremonton-Garland	435-257-7015
Hyrum North	435-245-4551	Tridell	435-247-2340
Kamas	435-783-2921	Valley Regional	801-378-6200
Kanab	435-644-5973	Vernal	435-789-3618
Kaysville East	801-543-2845	Wellington	435-637-6717
Kaysville South	801-543-2869	West Jordan Heritage	801-562-8285
Kearns Central	801-964-7470		

West Jordan Jordan Oak	801-280-4809
West Jordan Oquirrh	801-964-7332
West Jordan Prairie	801-964-7492
West Jordan Welby	801-280-4869

VERMONT

Bennington	802-447-1985
Montpelier	802-229-0482
Rutland	802-773-8346
South Royalton	802-763-7784

VIRGINIA

Albemarle	919-482-8688
Annandale	703-256-5518
Bennetts Creek	757-538-3610
Buckingham	804-969-2034
Buena Vista	540-261-6446
Centreville	703-830-5343
Charlottesville	804-975-3866
Chesapeake	757-482-9612
Danville	804-836-6212
Eastern Shore	757-787-4288
Fredericksburg	540-786-5641
Front Royal	540-636-9285
Gloucester	804-695-1162
Hamilton	540-338-9526
Harrisonburg	540-433-2945
Lynchburg	804-239-4744
Martinsville	540-629-7613
McLean	703-532-9019
Mt. Vernon	703-799-3071
New River	540-626-7264
Newport News	757-874-2335
Oakton	703-281-1836
Richmond	804-288-8134
Richmond Chesterfield	804-763-4318
Roanoke	540-562-2052
Tappahannock	804-443-3165
Beach Stk	757-467-3302
Warrenton	703-858-5930
Waynesboro	540-942-1036
Winchester	540-722-6055
Woodbridge	703-670-5977

WASHINGTON

Auburn	253-735-2009
Basin City	509-269-4237
Bellevue	425-454-2690
Bellevue North	425-562-0361
Bellingham	360-738-1849
Bremerton	360-479-9370
Bremerton 1st	360-895-3099
Brewster	509-689-3218
Centralia	360-748-1516
Chelan	509-682-5714
Colfax	509-397-2988
Colville	509-684-6642
Coulee Dam	509-633-1781
Davenport	509-725-0554
Dayton	509-382-2111
Elma	360-482-5982
Ephrata	509-754-4762
Everett	425-337-0457
Federal Way	253-874-3803
Goldendale	509-773-3824
Kennewick	509-627-0802
Kirkland	425-821-3939
Lacey	360-458-2460
Longview	360-577-8234
Lynnwood	425-776-6678
Maple Valley	425-413-7566
Morton	360-496-5959
Moses Lake	509-765-8711
Mount Vernon	360-424-7723
Ocean Shores	306-289-2037
Olympia	360-705-4176
Omak	509-826-4802
Oroville	509-476-2740
Othello	509-488-6412
Port Angeles	360-452-1521
Port Townsend	360-385-2604
Poulsbo	360-779-8655
Prosser	509-786-3860
Pullman	208-882-1769
Puyallup	253-863-3383
Puyallup South	253-840-1673
Quincy	509-787-2521
Raymond	360-942-3939
Redmond	425-881-7488
Renton North	425-888-1098
Richland	509-946-6637

Ritzville	509-659-0932	Fairmont	304-363-0116	Burlington	307-762-3204
Royal	509-346-2471	Franklin	304-358-7005	Casper	307-234-3326
San Juan	360-378-4162	Huntington	304-736-0250	Cheyenne	307-634-3561
Seattle	206-444-6017	Masontown	304-864-5377	Cody	307-587-3427
Seattle North	206-522-1233	Morgantown	304-594-1176	Cokeville	307-279-3266
Selah	509-925-5192	New Martinsville	304-455-1413	Douglas	307-358-5024
Selah South	509-697-9527	Parkersburg	304-428-2857	Dubois	307-455-3401
Shelton	360-427-9929			Evanston	307-789-2648
Silverdale	360-698-5552	**WISCONSIN**		Gillette	307-686-9177
Snohomish	425-334-0754	Appleton	920-733-5358	Glenrock	307-436-9619
Spokane	509-455-7164	Barron	715-537-3679	Green River	307-875-3972
Spokane East	509-926-0551	Eau Claire	715-834-8271	Jackson	307-733-6337
Spokane North	509-466-4633	Elkhorn	414-723-2777	Kemmerer	307-877-6821
Spokane West	509-455-9735	Green Bay	920-406-8050	Lander	307-332-5930
Stevenson	509-427-5927	Kenosha	414-552-7816	Laramie	307-745-3234
Sunnyside	509-837-5002	LaCrosse	608-783-3619	Lovell	307-548-2963
Tacoma	253-564-1103	Madison	608-238-4844	Lusk	307-334-2966
Vancouver	360-944-5773	Milwaukee	414-425-4182	Lyman	307-786-4559
Vancouver North	360-253-4701	Oshkosh	920-233-6545	Meeteetse	307-868-2424
Vancouver West	360-573-7881	Parkway	414-355-2241	Pinedale	307-369-4740
Vashon	206-463-1863	Shawano	715-526-2946	Powell	307-754-2110
Wahluke	509-932-4068	Sheboygan	920-452-7314	Rawlins	307-324-5459
Walla Walla	509-529-9211	Wausau	715-355-4856	Riverton	307-856-5290
Wenatchee	509-884-8686	West Bend	414-338-6123	Rock Springs	307-362-8062
Yakima	509-452-3626			Sheridan	307-672-8611
		WYOMING		Thermopolis	307-864-9452
WEST VIRGINIA		Afton	307-886-3905	Torrington	307-532-5862
Buckhannon	304-472-5213	Baggs	307-383-7695	Worland	307-347-8958
Charleston	304-984-9333	Basin-Greybull	307-568-2039		
Elkins	304-636-7750	Big Piney	307-276-3251		

INTERNATIONAL FAMILY HISTORY CENTERS

AUSTRALIA

NEW SOUTH WALES

Albury	02 6041 1883	Nambour	07 5441 6461	**WESTERN AUSTRALIA**	
Baulkham Hills	02 9686 7499	Oxley	07 3279 9936	Albany	08 9841 3641
Campbelltown	02 4626 7441	Redcliffe	07 3284 7196	Armadale	08 9497 2932
Carlingford	02 9872-8213	Rockhampton	07 4926 2455	Bridgetown	08 9761 2414
Coffs Harbour	02 6651 1254	Somerset	07 5465 6048	Bunbury	08 9721 4024
Cowra	02 6341 1306	Toowoomba	07 4635 5895	Dianella	08 9275 2608
Dapto	02 4261 6721	Townsville	07 4725 1681	Geraldton	08 9964 2832
Dubbo	02 6884 6016	Warwick	07 4661 5089	Green Mount	08 9294 3990
Emu Plains	02 4735 4640			Kalgoorlie	08 9021 1595
Finley	02 5883 1377	**SOUTH AUSTRALIA**		Karratha	08 9144 2364
Gosford	02 4328 4121	Berri	08 8582 2448	Melville	08 9330 3750
Grafton	02 6642 4148	Christies Beach	08 8384 5787	Narrogin	08 9881 2596
Greenwic	02 9436 0482	Elizabeth	08 8255 6413	Northam	08 9622 2472
Hebersham	02 9832-4318	Firle	08 8364 1488	Port Hedland	08 9172 3420
Leura	02 4784 2373	Fulham Gardens	08 8356 9977	Rockingham	08 9527 8846
Lismore	02 6624 1317	Marion	08 8276 7849	Warwick	08 9243 14292
Manly	02 9905 4484	Modbury	08 8263 1995		
Mittagong	02 4872 1212	Mount Gambier	08 8725 1613	**AUSTRIA**	
Mortdale	02 9570 6453	Port Augusta	08 8642 6492	Graz	43 316 58567
Newcastle	02 4942 3006	Port Pirie	08 633 0882	Innsbruck	0043 512342464
Nowra	02 4421 3244	Prospect	08 8344 2516	Klagenfurt	43 463 21130
Orange	02 6362 9192	Whyalla	08 8645 7354	Linz	43 732 42610
Parramatta	02 9630 1931			Salzburg	0043 662 825785
Prairiewood	02 9725 4410	**TASMANIA**		Vienna	43 1 729 6552
Richmond	02 4578 4599	Devonport	03 6427 9808	Wels	43 7242 63718
Sydney Hyde Park	02 9267 0898	Hobart	03 6273 3153		
Tamworth	02 6765 7051	Launceston	03 6344 7250	**BAHAMAS**	
Taree	02 6552 3653			Nassau	242 322-6618
Wagga Wagga	02 6925 2202	**VICTORIA**			
		Bairnsdale	03 5152 6692	**BELGIUM**	
NORTHERN TERRITORY		Ballarat	03 5338 2294	Antwerp	32 3646 0859
Alice Springs	08 8952 5871	Bendigo	03 5443 9536	Bruxelles	32 2537 3374
Darwin	08 8948 0818	Blackburn	03 9878 7414	Charleroi	32 7136 7644
		Braeside	03 9706 3205	Liege	32 4343 3463
QUEENSLAND		Caulfield	03 9576 1382	Namur	32 8130 1513
Atherton	07 4091 2059	Croydon	03 9725 5859		
Beenleigh	07 3207 7833	Deer Park	03 9363 7693	**BRAZIL**	
Brisbane	07 3391 7585	Epping	03 9401 4925	Alegrete	055 422-3904
Bundaberg	07 4153 1701	Fairfield	03 9482 6906	Americana	019 461-3524
Burpengary	07 3888 0084	Geelong	03 5278 1691	Anapolis	062 324-6004
Cairns	07 4053 1503	Goulburn Valley	03 5825 3547	Aracaju Bela Vista	079 231-7207
Charters Towers	07 4787 2524	Horsham	03 5382 4800	Aracaju Cidada Nova	079 222-9071
Dalby	07 4662 3288	Korumburra	03 5655 2433	Araraquara	016 236-9373
Eight Mile Plains	07 3341 0459	Maroondah	03 9887 3786	Bage	0532 42-1628
Enoggera	07 3855 2698	Mildura	03 5023 3576	Bauru	0142 22-6194
Gladstone	07 4979 2934	Moe	03 5127 3429	Belem	091 225-1374
Gold Coast	07 5531 5083	Moorabbin	03 9532 1596	Belem Cidade Nova	091 263-3659
Gympie	07 5482 2014	Pakenham	03 5941 4737	Belo Horizonte	031 223-7883
Hervey Bay	07 4124 1622	Sale	03 5144 6479	Birigui	018 642-1012
Ipswich	07 3201 5182	Seymour	03 5799 0177	Brasilia	061 245-1319
Kawana Waters	07 5493 3580	Sunbury	03 9740 8000	Brasilia Alvorada	062 628-1104
Kingaroy	07 4162 4676	Swan Hill	03 5032 2086	Litoral	085 236-1892
Mackay	07 4952 1974	Traralgon	03 5175 0170	Cachoeira do Sul	051 722-3463
Mount Isa	07 4743 4926	Wangaratta	03 5722 1112	Cachoeiro do Itapemirim Ward	027 522-0796
				Campina Grande	083 341-3420

When you have found a center near you, return to Step 3e on page 22.

Campinas	0192 32-4363
Campinas Castelo	0192 41-7545
Campinas Flamboyant	0192 32-0709
Campo Grande	067 761-1829
Canoas	051 472-8544
Caxias do Sul	054 221-1222
Contagem	031 351-4954
Cuiaba	065 321-2455
Curitiba	041 254-1684
Curitiba Boqueirao	041 276-6748
Curitiba Iguacu	041 335-5611
Curitiba Novo Mundo	041 247-3604
Curitiba Portao	041 345-2234
Curitiba Sao Lourenco	041 256-1632
Florianopolis	0482 23-4588
Fortaleza	085 272-6588
Fortaleza Bom Sucesso	085 245-1745
Fortaleza Montese	085 225-9722
Fortaleza Oeste	085 228-5107
Fortaleza Sul	085 291-1910
Foz do Iguacu	045 523-2378
Garanhuns	081 761-2169
Goiania	062 225-0211
Goiania Leste	062 223-9355
Gravatai	051470-2640
Guaratingueta	012 525-4688
Guaruja	013 386-5531
Ipatinga	031 822-2264
Itu	011 782-1048
Jaboatao Guararapes	081 341-7753
Joao Pessoa	083 231-2427
Joinville	0474 33-5519
Juiz de Fora	032 211-5567
Lages	0492 23-1288
Londrina Tiradentes	043 327-3017
Maceio	082 221-7739
Maceio Litoral	082 223-4476
Manaus	092 232-6944
Manaus Cidade Nova	092 221-5781
Manaus Rio Negro	092 233-4035
Marilia	0144 22-2793
Natal	084 223-2500
Nova Iguacu	021 768-2685
Novo Hamburgo	0512 93-7340
Olinda	081 431-1008
Olinda Paulista	081 433-0249
Osasco	011 702-4648
Passo Fundo	054 311-6188
Pelotas	0532 25-3000
Pelotas Norte	0532 23-4202
Petropolis	0242 42-5074
Piracicaba	019 421-0898
Pocos de Caldas Ward	035 721-5234
Ponta Grossa	0422 23-4267
Ponta Pora	067 431-4878
Porto Alegre	051 223-1219
Porto Alegre Moinhos Vento	051 222-2712
Porto Alegre Partenon	051 336-7234
Porto Alegre Sul	051 336-8022
Porto Velho	069 221-9989
Presidente Prudente	0182 33-4039
Recife	081 423-6162
Recife Boa Viagem	081 341-4333
Recife Caxangua	081-228-1505
Recife Imbiribeira	081 339-2929
Recife Jardim Sao Paulo	081251-4178
Ribeirao Pires	011 459-1748
Ribeirao Preto Centro	016 634-6826
Rio Branco	068 223-2280
Rio Claro	0195 24-2844
Rio de Janeiro	021 269-2245
Rio de Janeiro Andarai	021 268-4698
Rio de Janeiro Madureira	021 359-1511
Rio de Janeiro Niteroi	021 717-4151
Salvador	071 248-9552
Salvador Norte	071 234-3897
Santa Maria	055 221-4522
Santa Rita	083 232-1099
Santos	0132 32-3962
Sao Bernardo	011 457-7226
Sao Joao da Boa Vista	019 623-2509
Sao Jose	048 247-0385
Sao Jose dos Campos	0123 31-4399
Sao Luis	098 243-4912
Sao Paulo	011 818-0407
Sao Paulo Campo Limpo	011 491 6481
Sao Paulo Guarulhos	011 208 7114
Sao Paulo Interlagos	011 522 5525
Sao Paulo Ipiranga	011 272 4354
Sao Paulo Norte	011 298 7611
Sao Paulo Oeste	011 275-2607
Sao Paulo Parque Pinheiros	011 494-6539
Sao Paulo Penha	011 296-6888
Sao Paulo Perdizes	011 262-9004

Sao Paulo Piratininga	011 246-2675
Sao Paulo Pirituba	011 875-5974
Sao Paulo Sao Miguel	011 297-0879
Sao Paulo Taboao	011 815-0703
Sao Paulo Vila Sabrina	011 202-7583
Sao Vicente	013 468-0950
Sete Lagoas	031 921-4842
Sobradinho Ward	061 591-8967
Sorocaba	0152 21-5407
Teresina	086 222-3097
Uberlandia	034 217-0860
Uruguaiana	055 412-3646
Vila Velha	027 226-5268
Vitoria	027 225-6288

CANADA

ALBERTA

Barrhead	780-674-4208
Calgary	403-571-3700
Cardston	403-653-3288
Cherry Grove	780-594-3225
Coutts	403-344-3938
Drumheller	403-823-8824
EdmontonSt Paul	780-645-2337
Edmonton Bonnie Doon	780-469-6460
Edmonton Riverbend	780-436-0136
Fairview	403-835-3501
Fort Macleod	403-553-2556
Fort McMurray	780-790-9151
Grande Prairie	780-532-3609
Lethbridge	403-328-0206
Lloydminster	780-875-5727
Magrath	403-758-6472
Medicine Hat Stake	403-529-5131
Okotoks	403-938-4177
Olds	403-556-3043
Raymond-Magrath	403-752-4142
Red Deer	403-342-1508
Rocky Mountain House	403-845-6939
Rosemary	403-378-4478
Taber	403-223-9066

BRITISH COLUMBIA

100 Mile House	250-395-2421
Abbotsford	604-852-8043
Burns Lake	250-695-6316
Campbell River	250-287-3858
Chetwynd	250-788-9127
Courtenay	250-334-2523
Cranbrook	250-426-4614
Creston	250-428-7919
Duncan	250-746-4122
Fort St. John	250-785-4351
Kamloops	250-376-2515
Kelowna	250-762-0588
Kitimat	250-632-4720
Nanaimo Stake	250-758-1360
Nelson	250-352-5310
North Island	250-956-4125
Penticton	250-493-5580
Port Alberni	250-723-9377
Powell River	604-485-9446
Prince George	250-563-1490
Prince Rupert BC	250-624-2354
Qualicum	250-752-2233
Quesnel	250-747-2422
Salmon Arm	250-832-4085
Smithers	250-847-9802
Sparwood	250-425-0523
Surrey	604-597-9695
Terrace	250-635-9263
Trail	250-368-6616
Vancouver BC 1st Ward	604-324-4338
Vancouver	604-299-8656
Vanderhoof	250-567-9796
Vernon	250-545-1283
Victoria	250-479-3631
Williams Lake	250-392-4271

MANITOBA

Brandon	204-728-3935
Flin Flon	204-687-4028
Thompson	204-677-4060
Winnipeg	204-261-4271

NEW BRUNSWICK

Moncton	506-856-8909
Saint John	506-672-0864

NEWFOUNDLAND

Corner Brook	709-634-9700
St Johns	709-368-2601

NOVA SCOTIA

Bridgewater	902-543-2099
Dartmouth	902-462-0628
New Glasgow	902-928-0916

ONTARIO

Bancroft	613-332-9878
Barrie	705-722-9152
Black Creek	416-242-7392
Bracebridge	705-645-3262
Brampton	905-799-3214
Brantford	519-753-3725
Brockville	613-345-0410
Burlington	905-335-4733
Cambridge	519-622-0092
Campbellford	705-653-5233
Chatham	519-352-4627
Cornwall	613-933-1716
Dryden	807-937-5289
Fort Frances	807-274-9394
Hamilton	905-385-5009
Kenora	807-548-5097
Kingston	613-544-8489
Kitchener	519-741-9591
London	519-473-2421
McCowan	416-422-5480
Mississauga	416-621-4607
North Bay	705-474-9205
Oshawa	905-728-3151
Ottawa	613-224-2231
Owen Sound	519-376-2482
Petawawa	613-687-2237
Peterborough	705-745-8912
Sarnia	519-542-7126
Sault Ste. Marie	705-254-5892
Simcoe	519-428-2310
Smiths Falls	613-283-8320
St Catharines	905-685-5795
St Thomas	519-631-2641
Sudbury	705-264-8990
Sudbury Ward	705-560-2613
Temiskaming	705-672-2057
Thunder Bay	807-683-8727
Toronto	416-422-5480
Trenton	613-392-5381
Walkerton	519-881-2473
Windsor	519-735-4433
Woodstock	519-537-3121

PRINCE EDWARD ISLAND

Charlottetown	902-566-1013

QUEBEC

Drummondville	819-478-8554
Gatineau	819-561-2442
Montreal	514-523-6131
Montreal Mt Royal	514-367-1615
Quebec Canada District	418-871-7771
Rimouski Quebec	418-722-6721

SASKATCHEWAN

Kindersley	306-463-4808
Moose Jaw	306-692-3246
Prince Albert	306-763-7874
Regina	306-543-2782
Saskatoon	306-343-6060
Whitehorse Yukon	867-668-7961

DENMARK

Aalburg	45 9813 1157
Aarhus	45 8614 1584
Copenhagen	45 3834 5570
Esbjerg	45 7512 2375
Fredericia	45 4 7591 2672
Frederikshavn	45 9842 7733
Odense	45 6617 8674
Slagelse	45 5352 6837

DOMINICAN REPUBLIC

Oriental	809-592-6332
San Francisco de Macoris	809-244-1855
San Geromino	809-567-3704
Santiago	809-241-2050
Santo Domingo	809-682-4779

ENGLAND

Aldershot	01252 21460
Ashton	0161 330 3453
Billingham	01325 566412
Birkenhead	0151 608 7723
Blackpool	01253 858218
Bristol	01225 777097
Cambridge	01223 247010

Canterbury	01227 765431
Carlisle	01228 26767
Cheltenham	01242 523433
Chorley	01257 226199
Coventry	01203 301420
Crawley	01293 520639
Exeter	01392 50723
Forest of Dean	01594 832904
Gillingham	1634 230357
Grimsby	01472 828876
Harborne	0121 553 2137
Hastings	01424 754563
Helston	01326 564503
Hereford	01432 352751
Huddersfield	01484 454573
Hull	01482 701439
Ipswich	01473 723182
King's Lynn	01553 670000
Lancaster	01524 33571
Leeds	01132 585297
Leicester	00 44 1162 737334
Lichfield	01543 414843
Lincoln	01522 680117
Liverpool	0151 252 0614
London Hyde Park	0171 589 8561
London Wandsworth	0181 673 6741
Lowestoft	01502 573851
Macclesfield	1625 427236
Maidstone	01622 757811
Manchester	0161 902-9279
Mansfield	01623 26729
Newcastle-Under-Lyme	01782 614042
Newport	01983 529643
Northampton	01604 751348
Norwich	01603 452440
Nottingham	0115 914 4255
Orpington	01689 837342
Peterborough	01733 263374
Plymouth	01752 668666
Pontefract	01977 600308
Poole	01202 730646
Portsmouth	01705 696243
Preston	44-125 7226145
Rawtenstall	01706 213460
Reading	0118 942 7524
Redditch	01527 550657
Romford	01708 620727
Scarborough	01723 501026
Sheffield	0114 245-3124
St Albans	01582 482234
St Helier	00 3531 341737
St Austell	01726 69912
Staines	01784 462627
Stevenage	01438 351553
Sunderland	01915 285787
Sutton Coldfield	0121 386 1690
Telford	01952 257443
Thetford	01842 755472
Watford	1923 251471
Wednesfield	01902 724097
Worthing	01903 241829
Yate	01454 323004
Yeovil	01935 26817
York	01904 785128

FINLAND

Hameenlinna	9358 176824391
Helsinki	9358 0578963
Helsinki	9358 03432235
Hyvinkaa	9358 14484088
Jyvaskyla	9358 41615274
Kemi	9358 16255001
Kerava	9358 0248127
Kuopio	9358 712622619
Lahti	9358 187526445
Lappeenranta	9358 534150129
Mikkeli	9358 55211103
Oulu	9358 8335714
Pietarsaari	9358 677230147
Pori	9358 396355216
Rauma	9358 388250796
Rovaniemi	9358 6020401
Tampere	9358 32554485
Turku	9358 2135644
Vaasa	9358 61175215

FRANCE

Arras	33 21 73 88 89
Bayonne	33 5 59 638 62 04
Bergerac	33 53 61 37 31
Besancon	0033-381-632781
Bordeaux	33 5 56 80 70 14
Caen	33 2 31 83 09 88
Calais	33 3 21 96 85 45
Cannes	33 4 93 69 84 26
Carcassonne	33 4 68 71 39 30
Castres	33 5 63 59 19 33

Chalon-sur-Soane	33 3 8543 2090
Chambery	33 4 79 69 05 85
Charleville-Mezieres	33 3 24 59 38 24
Clermont-Ferrand	33 4 73 27 50 36
Compiegne	33 3 44 86 02 85
Dijon	33 3 80 41 28 87
Dunkerque	33 3 28 60 51.36
Grenoble	33 4 76 21 77 27
Le Havre	33 2 35 43 48 87
Le Mans	33 2 43 81 14 40
Lille	33 3 20 47 12 61
Limoges	33 5 55 05 11 44
Lyon	33 4 78 33 00 74
Marseille Borely	33 4 91 76 17 31
Meaux	33 1 60 04 65 23
Metz	33 3 87 36 82 35
Montpelier	33 4 67 07 93 19
Mulhouse	33 3 89 50 17 25
Nancy	33 3 83 96 39 22
Nantes	33 2 40 49 23 17
Nice	33 4 93 81 69 69
Nimes	33 4 66 29 40 14
Nogent	33 1 48 76 31 64
Orleans	33 2 38 43 75 09
Paris Cergy	33 1 34 24 85 38
Paris East	33 1 42 45 29 29
Pau	33 5 59 62 70 62
Perigueux	3 3 55 53 03 98 85
Perpignan	33 4 68 67 45 08
Reims	33 3 26 06 03 69
Rennes	33 2 99 83 34 27
Rouen	33 2 35 71 79 21
Saint Die	33 3 29 55 05 73
Saint-Etienne	33 4 77 37 83 88
Saint Quentin	33 3 23 64 74 65
Strasbourg	33 3 88 18 87 62
Toul	33 3 83 43 40 42
Toulon	33 4 94 20 13 38
Toulouse	33 5 56 11 92 81
Tours	33 2 47 53 28 44
Troyes	33 3 25 81 21 71
Valence	33 4 75 42 90 38
Valenciennes	33 3 27 29 94 54
Versailles	33 1 39 55 39 14

GERMANY

Aachen	49 241 76494
Altona	49 40 8806412
Annaberg-Buchholz	49 373 33416
Augsburg	49 821 574606
Baumholder	49 6783 980565
Berlin	49 30 262 1088
Bielefeld	49 521-881966
Bitburg	49 6561 4836
Bonn	49 228 645978
Braunschweig	49 531 55322
Brandenburg	49 3381 24379
Bremen	49 421 223 8557
Bremerhaven	49 471 88937
Celle	49 5141 23447
Coburg	49 9561 10643
Darmstadt	49 6151 718429
Dortmund	49 231 714492
Dresden	49 351 471 5333
Duisburg	49 203 314301
Dusseldorf	49 211 625846
Ellwangen	49 7961 52357
Erfurt	49 361 2252741
Esslingen	49 711 3166635
Forst	49 3562 984081
Frankfurt	49 69 546005
Frankfurt Hochst	49 69 345990
Freiburg	43 0761 492688
Freiberg	49 3731 359620
Friedrichsdorf	49 6172 72096
Goppingen	49 7161 84403
Gottingen	49 551 63918
Halle	49 345 6950039
Hamburg	49 40 2619 8959
Hanau	49 6181 12280
Hannover	49 511 8699722
Heidelberg	49 6221 401884
Heilbronn	49 7131 44520
Kaiserslautern	49 631 95245
Karlsruhe	49 721 815698
Kassel	49 561 26543
Kaufbeuren	49 8341 68510
Kiel	49 431 91733
Koblenz	49 261 17747
Hamm	49 2381-789029
Koln	49 221 979 2053 + 54
Krefeld	49 2151 399227
Landshut	49 871 78541
Langen	49 6103 22649
Langenhorn	49 40 5207273

Leer	49 491 67870
Leipzig	49 341 4793948
Lubeck	49 451 34356
Ludwigsburg	49 7141 75877
Mannheim	49 621 7425080
Michelstadt	49 6061 73757
Minden	49 571 46784
Monchengladbach	49 2162 206402
Munich	49 89 5380873
Neubrandenburg	49 395 5841790
Neumuenster	49 4321 38548
Nurnberg	49 911 533990
Offenburg	49 781 36523
Oldenburg	49 441 776991
Osnabruck	49 541 803293
Paderborn	49 5251 61850
Passau	49 85175 61036
Pinneberg	4101 29809
Regensburg	49 89 560831
Rosenheim	49 8031 42763
Rahlstedt	49 40 6791444
Rheinpfalz	49 6236 61927
Rostock	49 381 2005880
Saarbrucken	49 681 44837
Schwenningen	49 7720 5655
Schwerin	49 385 568361
Singen	43 07731 60446
Spandau	49 30 375 2194
Stade	49 4141 2879
Stadthagen	49 5721 3130
Stuttgart	49 711-2572118
Stuttgart Happel	49 711 8893910
Trier	49 651 74577
Ulm	49 731 87602
Unna	49 02303-54151
Waiblingen	49 7151 18674
Wetterau	49 6034 3108
Wetzlar	49 6441 77770
Wiesbaden	49 0611 841833
Wilhelmshaven	49 4421 37250
Wolfsburg	49 5361 291504
Wolgast	49 38 366 00444
Wuppertal	49 0202-87207
Wurzburg	49 931 284866
Zwickau	49 375 785282

GUAM

Micronesia	671-734-3565

HONG KONG

Hong Kong Island	852-547-6284

HUNGARY

Budapest	0036-1-1353698

ICELAND

Reykjavik	9354 5528730

INDONESIA

Jakarta	011-6221-726-2612

IRELAND

Cork	010 3531 306637
Dublin	010 3531 830 9960

ISLE OF MAN

Douglas	01624 675834

ITALY

Alessandria	39 131 264302
Agrigento Sicily	39 91 341001
Bergamo	39 35 401772
Brescia	39 30 312156
Bolzano	39 471 930780
Catania	39 95 7125128
Como	39 31 505032
Firenze	39 055 4222403
Foggia	39 881 742582
Genova	39 10 532741
La Spezia	39 187 517893
Livorno	39 586 857554
Messina Sicily	39 90 718029
Milano	39 22 847416
Modena	39 59 370745
Napoli	39 81 5490012
Pescara	39 85 377107
Piacenza	39 523 388408
Pordenone	39 434 31727
Rimini	39 541 750375
Roma	39 66 7182113
Trieste	39 40 946521
Palermo	39 91 341001
Pisa	39 50 530136

When you have found a center near you, return to Step 3e on page 22

Ragusa	39 932 642004
Sardegna	39 70 530043
Sassari	39 79 237805
Siracusa	39 931 69980
Taranto	39 99 7796738
Torino	39 11 251669
Trapani	39 923 563622
Venezia	39 41 98181
Vercelli	39 161 51771
Verona	39 45 521088

JAPAN

Okinawa Servicemen	819-8892-8913

MEXICO

Acapulco	01 74 83 52 78
Atlixco	01 244 5 35 45
Campeche	01 981 6 17 48
Cancun	01 98 87 71 45
Chalco	01 597 3 01 02
Chihuahua	14-13-11-92
Chetumal	01 983 2 99 67
Ciudad Obregon Nainari	641 31017
Coatzacoalcos	01 921 5 31 77
Colonia Dublan	4-00-82
Cuautla	01 735 3 80 25
Jalapa	01 28 18 20 66
Juchitan	01 971 1 02 60
Los Mochis	5 10 33
Merida Lakin	01 99 21 88 20
Mexico City Aragon	7 47 48 31 x3330
Mexico City Camarones	5 56 13 74
Mexico City Contreras	5 73 58 21
Mexico City Cuautitlan	8 73 95 13
Mexico City Ecatepec	7 70 09 47
Mexico City Ermita	6 72 25 36
Mexico City Industrial	5 37 19 85
Mexico City La Perla	7 33 96 33
Mexico City Lindavista	7 54 47 09
Mexico City Meyehualco	6 91 56 08
Mexico City Netzahualcoyotl	7 44 88 03
Mexico City Tlalnepantla	3 90 81 76
Mexico City Tlalpan	5 94 96 29
Mexico City Valle Dorado	3 70 90 25
Mexico City Villa de las Flores	874 36 08
Mexico City Zarahemla	7 26 45 00
Monclova	3-24-32
Monterrey Roma	387 22 90
Nuevo Laredo	13 48 42
Oaxaca	01 951 3 00 28
Orizaba	01 272 5 58 80
Papantla	01 784 2 35 501
Poza Rica Palmas	01 782 2 08 06
Puebla Cholula	01 22 47 26 73
Puebla Fuertes	01 22 46 66 47
Puebla La Paz	01 22 48 18 01
Puebla Nealtican	01 22 8 00 46
Queretaro	01 42 15 28 03
Tapachula	01 962 6 22 23
Tapachula Izapa	01 962 5 09 05
Tecalco	01 597 6 07 70
Tlaxcala	01 246 7 23 30
Toluca	01 72 19 64 21
Tula	01 773 2 24 18
Veracruz Reforma	01 29 31 28 49
Villahermosa	01 93 13 42 66

NETHERLANDS

Amsterdam	31 20 6944990
Apeldoorn	31 555 521 7516
Breda	31 76 5213141
Den Haag	31 70 3211156
Den Helder	31 223 623074
Dordrecht	31 78 6135537
Eindhoven	31 40 423526
Gouda	31 182 518512
Groningen	31 50 5256271
Heerlen Servicements	31 45 717863
Leeuwarden	31 58 2135361
Rotterdam	31 10 4149883
Utrecht	31 30 2444218

NEW CALEDONIA

New Caledonia	687 285 548

NEW ZEALAND

Auckland Harbour	09 486 2302
Blenheim	03 578 7235
Christchurch	03 355 6874
Dunedin	03 455 3507
Gisborne	06 867 0941
Greymouth	03 768 9357
Hamilton	07 849 1758
Hastings	06 879 9320
Henderson	09 818 7898
Hibiscus	09 426 6725

Invercargill	03 215 7682
Kaikohe	09 405 2645
Kawhia	07 871 0732
Manukau	09 275 1170
Manurewa	09 267 5479
Masterton	06 377 3688
Mt. Roskill	09 625 9669
Nelson	03 547 9507
New Plymouth	06 758 9646
Paeroa	07 862 7690
Palmerston	06 355 1677
Panmure	09 535 2118
Rotorua	07 348 8129
Taumarunui	07 895 5400
Tauranga	07 578 7607
Temple View	07 847 4326
Timaru	03 686 0931
Tokoroa	07 886 6945
Porirua	04 237 5412
Tamaki	09 276 5189
Upper Hutt	04 526 4259
Wairoa	06 838 7982
Wanganui	06 344 5805
Wellington	04 386 1273
Whakatane	07 307 1166
Whangarei	09 437 2621

NORWAY

Bergen	947 55910510
Drammen	947 32822943
Fredrikstad	947 69397285
Kristiansand	947 38026455
Moss	947 69275455
Oslo	947 22384314
Skien	947 73523143
Stavanger	947 51589977
Trondheim	947-73513845

PHILIPPINES

Cabuyao	566-2456
Caloocan	362-28-85
Legaspi	52-80
Makati	88-92-92
Ozamiz	21326 or 20605
Zamboanga	991-2513

PORTUGAL

Alverca	351 1 9584919
Angra do Heroismo	351 95 628477
Barreiro	351 1 2156603
Coimbra	351 39 718437
Faro	351 89 801488
Lisboa	351 1 8463067
Madeira	351 91 236860
Matosinhos	351 2 6172850
Miratejo	351 1 2552222
Oeiras	351 1 4437727
Ovar	351 56 575470
Ponta Delgada	351 96 26409
Portimao	351 82 84544
Porto	351 2 520748
Setubal	351 65 772693
Viseu	351 32 425559

PUERTO RICO

Caguas District	809-738-0581
Carolina	809-769-5180
Fajardo	787-860-5235
Mayaguez	787-832-6026
Ponce	787-840-0219
San Juan	809-748-0630

SCOTLAND

Aberdeen	01224 692206
Dumfries	01387 254865
Dundee	01382 451247
Edinburgh	0131 337 3049
Elgin	01343 546429
Glasgow	0141 357 1024
Inverness	01463 231220
Kilmarnock	01563 26560
Kirkcaldy	01592 640041
Lerwick	01595 695732
Paisley	0141 884 2780

SINGAPORE

Singapore	011-65-735-5323

SPAIN

Albacete	0034-96-7247630
Alcala de Henares	34 918 812953
Alcoy	34 967 247630
Algeciras	34 95 6604618
Alicante	34 965 247008

Asturias	34 985 563581
Bilbao	34 944 240181
Badajoz	34 93 3990751
Badalona	34 933 990751
Barcelona	34 932 108353
Cadiz	34 956 594029
Cartagena	34 968 503834
Cornella	34 934 733148
Elche	34 965 421141
Gijon	34 985 130096
Granada	34 95 8126101
Jaen	34 953 275149
La Coruna	34 981 152746
La Palmas de Gran Canaria	34 928 242735
Madrid	34 915 343416
Mostoles	34 916 642712
Malaga	34 952 240515
Murcia	34 968 503834
Oviedo	34 985 275667
Pamplona	34 948 175887
Pontevedra	34 986 862117
Reus	34 977 316705
Sabadell	34 937 268161
Santa Cruz de Tenerife	34 922 240387
Sevilla	34 954 377753
Tarragona	34 977 241920
Torrejon de Ardos	34 916 773091
Valencia	34 963 934803
Valladolid	34 983 374657
Vilafranca	34 938 171124
Vitoria	34 945 262193
Zaragoza	34 976 389806

SWEDEN

Alingsas	46 0322 14918
Boras	46 033 129744
Borlange	46 0243 15119
Falun	46 023 10315
Gavle	46 026 511663
Hagersten	46 08 7443185
Helsingborg	46 042 123046
Jonkoping	46 036 710781
Karlskrona	46 0455-29132
Lulea	46 0920 225154
Orebro	46 019 254870
Skelleftea	46 0910 53046
Skovde	46 0500 85528
Sodertalje	46 08 55011130
Sundsvall	46 060 500350
Trollhattan	49 0520 16742
Umea	46 090 196021
Vasterhaninge	46 08 50065590
Vastra Frolunda	46 031 456692

SWITZERLAND

Annemasse Switzerland	3 4 5038 9715
Ebnat	41 74 9331270
Geneva	41 22 7986357
Kreuzlingen	41 71 6724828
Lausanne	41 21 6530134
Lugano	41 91 9401052
Luzern	41 41 3602905
Neuchatel	41 38 314100
Pratteln	41 61 8210031
Renens	41 21 6347934
St. Gallen	41 71 312174
Wettingen	41 56 4262304
Winterthur	41 52 2325229
Yverdon	41 24 211320
Zollikofen	41 31 9114799
Zurich	41 1 3228301

TONGA

Nuku' Alofa	41-055

URUGUAY

Melo	059 642-3234
Montevideo Oeste	984-709
Montevideo Cerro	373401
Paysandu	22522
Rivera	0598 622-2417

WALES

Cardiff	01222 620205
Gaerwen	1248 421894
Merthyr Tydfil	01685 722455
Newcastle Emlyn	01559 370945
Rhyl	01745 331172
Swansea	01792 585792

MAJOR U.S. GENEALOGICAL LIBRARIES

Allen County Public Library
Fred J. Reynolds Historical Genealogy Collection - contains family histories, census records, city directories, passenger lists, military records, U.S. Local Records, Native American and African American Records, and the largest English-language genealogy and local history periodical collection in the world.
900 Webster St,
Fort Wayne, IN 46802
Phone: 219-421-1200
Web: <www.acpl.lib.in.us/genealogy/genealogy.html>

American Genealogical Lending Library (Heritage Quest) -
Advertises having the nation's largest private microfilm collection. Contains over 250,000 titles -- including the entire U.S. Census collection, that are available for purchase or rental
(mailing address)
PO Box 329
Bountiful, Utah 84011-0329
Phone: 1-800-760-2455 ext. 523
Web:

Bancroft Library -
contains large collection of Western North American history
University of California Berkeley
Berkeley, CA 94720-6000
Phone: 510-642-3781
Web: <http://library.berkeley.edu/BANC/index.html>

Library of Congress -
Genealogical Room - contains resources from around the world.
Thomas Jefferson Annex,
101 Independence Ave. S.E.
Washington, D.C. 20540
Phone: 202-707-5000
Web: <http://lcweb.loc.gov/>

Newberry Library -
contains colonial America genealogies, local histories of U.S., indexes, abstracts or transcriptions of pre-twentieth century records,
60 W. Walton Street
Chicago, IL 60610

Phone: 312-943 9090
Web:<www.newberry.org/nl/newberryhome.html>

New York City Public Library
Local History and Genealogy
Division - contains materials documenting American History on the national, state and local level, Genealogy, Heraldry, Personal and Family Names, and Flags. Genealogical materials are international in scope, including foreign language materials in roman alphabets.
Fifth Avenue & 42nd Street
New York, NY 10018-2788
Phone: (212) 930-0830
Web: <www.nypl.org/research/chss/index.html>

Sutro Library -
referred to as "the largest genealogical library west of Salt Lake City," contains genealogy, local history, city directories, ship manifests and census collections for most states.
480 Winston Dr.
San Francisco, CA 94132
Phone: 415-731-4477
Web: <www.records.org/sutro.html>

U.S. NATIONAL ARCHIVES AND RECORDS ADMINISTRATION (NARA)

Archives -
The following list of state offices of vital records was taken from information published by the U.S. Government Printing Office - Where to Write for Vital Records - Births, Deaths, Marriages and Divorces. Family History SourceGuideTM - How-to Guides Version of Data: March 1998.
<http://32.96.111.5/sg/WheToWri.html>
Call the agency you're interested in before writing for records. To obtain a certified copy of any of the certificates, write or go to the vital statistics office in the State or area where the event occurred.

Archives I -
in Washington, DC , contains textual and microfilm records relating to genealogy, American Indians, pre-World War II military and naval-maritime matters, the New Deal, the District of Columbia, the Federal courts, and Congress.
700 Pennsylvania Avenue, N.W.
Washington, D.C. 20408
Web: <www.nara.gov/index.html>

Archives II -
at College Park, Maryland contains special media and nontextual records, such as cartographic and architectural records, motion pictures, audio recordings, videocassettes, still pictures, and electronic records.
National Archives at College Park
8601 Adelphi Road
College Park, MD 20740-6001 Web:
<www.nara.gov/nara/dc/Archives2_directions.html>
Archives II is located near the University of Maryland's College Park campus.

Washington National Records Center -
Contains holdings for Federal agency headquarters offices in the District of Columbia, Maryland, and Virginia; Federal agency field offices in Maryland, Virginia, and West Virginia; Federal courts in the District of Columbia; and U.S. Armed Forces worldwide.
4205 Suitland Road
Suitland, Maryland 20746-8001
Phone: 301-457-7000
Web: <www.nara.gov/records/wnrc.html>

National Personnel Records Center (St. Louis) -
Contains civilian personnel records from Federal agencies nationwide; selected military dependent medical records.
Civilian Personnel Records
111 Winnebago Street
St. Louis, Missouri 63118-4199
Web: <www.nara.gov/regional/cpr.html>

National Personnel Records Center (St. Louis) -
contains military personnel records, and military and retired military medical records from all services; selected dependent medical records, morning reports, rosters, and Philippine army and guerilla records.
Military Personnel Records
9700 Page Avenue
St. Louis, Missouri 63132-5100
Web: <www.nara.gov/regional/mpr.html>

U.S. NATIONAL ARCHIVES AND RECORDS ADMINISTRATION - BRANCHES

Central Plains Region (Kansas City) -
contains holdings from Federal agencies and courts in Iowa, Kansas, Missouri and Nebraska.
2312 East Bannister Road
Kansas City, Missouri 64131-3011
Phone: 816-926-6272
Web: <www.nara.gov/regional/kansas.html>

Central Plains Region (Lee's Summit) -
contains holdings from Federal agencies and courts in New Jersey, New York, Puerto Rico, and the U.S. Virgin Islands, and from most Department of Veterans Affairs and Immigration and Naturalization Service offices nationwide.
200 Space Center Drive
Lee's Summit, Missouri 64064-1182
Phone: 816-478-7079
Web: <www.nara.gov/regional/leesumit.html>

Great Lakes Region (Chicago) -
contains holdings from Federal agencies and courts in Illinois, Indiana, Michigan, Minnesota, Ohio, and Wisconsin.
7358 South Pulaski Road
Chicago, Illinois 60629-5898
Phone: 773-581-7816
Web: <www.nara.gov/regional/chicago.html>

Great Lakes Region (Dayton) -
contains holdings from Federal agencies in Indiana, Michigan, and Ohio; Federal bankruptcy court records from Ohio since 1991/92; Defense Finance Accounting System records nationwide and from Germany and Korea; and Internal Revenue Service records from selected sites nationwide.
3150 Springboro Road
Dayton, Ohio 45439-1883
Phone: 937-225-2852
Web: <www.nara.gov/regional/dayton.html>

Mid Atlantic Region (Center City Philadelphia) -
contains holdings from Federal agencies and courts in Delaware, Maryland, Pennsylvania, Virginia, and West Virginia.
900 Market Street
Philadelphia, Pennsylvania 19107-4292
Phone: 215-597-3000
Web: <www.nara.gov/regional/philacc.html>

Mid Atlantic Region (Northeast Philadelphia) -
contains holdings from Federal agencies in Delaware and Pennsylvania and Federal courts in Delaware, Maryland, Pennsylvania, Virginia, and West Virginia.
14700 Townsend Road
Philadelphia, Pennsylvania 19154-1096
Phone: 215-671-9027
Web: <www.nara.gov/regional/philane.html>

Northeast Region (Boston) -
contains holdings from Federal agencies and courts in Connecticut, Maine, Massachusetts, New Hampshire, Rhode Island, and Vermont.
380 Trapelo Road
Waltham, Massachusetts 02452-6399
Phone: 781-647-8104
Web: <www.nara.gov/regional/boston.html>

Northeast Region (New York City) -
contains holdings from Federal agencies and courts in New Jersey, New York, Puerto Rico, and the U.S. Virgin Islands.
201 Varick Street
New York, New York 10014-4811
Phone: 212-337-1300
Web: <www.nara.gov/regional/newyork.html>

Northeast Region (Pittsfield) -
contains holdings from selected Federal agencies nationwide.
10 Conte Drive
Pittsfield, Massachusetts 01201-8230
Phone: 413-445-6885
Web: <www.nara.gov/regional/pittsfie.html>

Pacific Alaska Region (Anchorage) -
contains holdings from Federal agencies and courts in Alaska.
654 West Third Avenue
Anchorage, Alaska 99501-2145
Phone: 907-271-2441
Web: <www.nara.gov/regional/anchorag.html>

Pacific Region (Laguna Niguel) -
contains holdings from Federal agencies and courts in Arizona, southern California, and Clark County, Nevada.
24000 Avila Road, First Floor-East Entrance
Laguna Niguel, California 92677-3497
P. O. Box 6719
Laguna Niguel, California 92607-6719
Phone: 949-360-2641
Web: <www.nara.gov/regional/laguna.html>

Pacific Region (San Francisco) -
contains holdings from Federal agencies and courts in northern California, Hawaii, Nevada (except Clark County), the Pacific Trust Territories, and American Samoa.
1000 Commodore Drive
San Bruno, California 94066-2350
Phone: 650-876-9009
Web: <www.nara.gov/regional/sanfranc.html>

Rocky Mountain Region (Denver) -
contains holdings from Federal agencies and courts in Colorado, Montana, New Mexico, North Dakota, South Dakota, Utah, and Wyoming.
Building 48, Denver Federal Center
West 6th Ave. and Kipling St.
Denver, Colorado 80225
Phone: 303-236-0804
Web: <www.nara.gov/regional/denver.html>

Southeast Region (Atlanta (East Point)] -
contains holdings from Federal agencies and courts in Alabama, Florida, Georgia, Kentucky, Mississippi, North Carolina, South Carolina, and Tennessee.
1557 St. Joseph Avenue
East Point, Georgia 30344-2593
Phone: 404-763-7474
Web: <www.nara.gov/regional/atlanta.html>

Southwest Region (Fort Worth) -
contains holdings from Federal agencies and courts in Arkansas, Louisiana, Oklahoma, and Texas.
501 West Felix Street, Building 1
Fort Worth, Texas 76115-3405
P. O. Box 6216
Fort Worth, Texas 76115-0216
Phone: 817-334-5525
Web: <www.nara.gov/regional/ftworth.html>

When you have found a library or archive near you, return to Step 3e on page 22

PLACES WHERE RECORDS ARE STORED

U.S. OFFICES OF STATE VITAL RECORDS

ALABAMA
Bureau of Vital Statistics Department of Public Health
Montgomery, AL 36130
(205) 261-5033
BIRTH and DEATH: State has records since January 1908.

ALASKA
Alaska Department of Health Bureau of Vital Statistic
Pouch H-02G
Juneau, AK 99811
(907) 465-3391
BIRTH, DEATH and MARRIAGE: State office has records since 1913.

ARIZONA
Division of Vital Records State Department of Health
P.O Box 3887
Phoenix, AZ 85030
(602) 255-1080
BIRTH and DEATH: State office has records since July 1909.

ARKANSAS
Division of Vital Records Arkansas Department of Health
4815 W. Markham St.
Little Rock, AR 72201
Phone: 501-661-2336
BIRTH and DEATH: State has records since February 1914. Some records from Little Rock and Fort Smith date back to 1881.

CALIFORNIA
Vital Statistic Branch Department of Health Services
410 N St.
Sacramento, CA 95814
Phone: 916-445-2684.
BIRTH, DEATH and MARRIAGE: State has records since July 1905. Check the county Recorder's office in county where the event occurred.

COLORADO
Vital Records Section Colorado Department of Health
4210 E. 11th Ave.
Denver, CO 80220
Phone: 303-320-8333
BIRTH and DEATH: State has birth records since 1910. Death records go back to 1900.

CONNECTICUT
Department of Health Services Vital Records Section Division of Health Statistics
150 Washington St.
Hartford, CT 06106
Phone: 203-566-1124
BIRTH and DEATH: State has records since July 1897. For earlier records, write the Registrar of Vital Statistics in the town where the event occurred.

DELAWARE
Office of Vital Statistics Division of Public Health
P.O. Box 637
Dover, DE 19903
Phone: 302-736-4721
BIRTH and DEATH: State has records for 1861-63 and from 1881 to the present, but no records for 1864-1880.

DISTRICT OF COLUMBIA
Vital Records Section
425 I St. N.W. Room 3009
Washington, D.C. 20001
Phone: 202-727-5316
BIRTH AND DEATH: State has birth records since 1871 and death records since 1855, but no death records filed during the Civil War.

FLORIDA
Department of Health and Rehabilitative Services Office of Vital Statistics
P.O. Box 210
Jacksonville, FL 32231
Phone: 904-359-6900
BIRTH AND DEATH: Most records date from 1917, although state has some birth records since April 1865 and some death records since August 1877.

GEORGIA
Department of Human Resources Vital Records Unit,
Room 217-H 47 Trinity Ave. S.W.
Atlanta, GA 30334
Phone: 404-656-4900
BIRTH AND DEATH: State has records since January 1919. Atlanta and Savannah have some earlier records available from the county.

HAWAII
Research and Statistics Office State Department of Health
Honolulu, HA 96801
Phone: 808-548-5819
BIRTH and DEATH: State has records since 1853.

IDAHO
Bureau of Vital Statistics State Department of Health
Statehouse
Boise, ID 83720
Phone: 208-334-5988
BIRTH and DEATH: State has records since 1911. County Recorder where event occurred has earlier records.

ILLINOIS
Division of Vital Records State Department of Health
605 West Jefferson St.
Springfield, IL 62702
Phone: 217-782-6553
BIRTH and DEATH: State has records since January 1916. County Clerk in county where event occurred has earlier records.

INDIANA
Division of Vital Records State Board of Health
1330 West Michigan St. P.O. Box 1964
Indianapolis, IN 46206
Phone: 317-633-0274
BIRTH and DEATH: State has birth records since October 1907 and death records since 1900. Health Officer in city or county where event occurred has earlier records.

IOWA
Department of Public Health Vital Records Section
Lucas Office Building
Des Moines, IA 50319
Phone: 515-281-5871
BIRTH, DEATH and MARRIAGE: State has records since July 1889.

KANSAS
Office of Vital Statistics Kansas State Department of Health and Environment
900 Jackson St.
Topeka, KN. 66612
Phone: 913-296-1400
BIRTH and DEATH: State has records since July 1911. County Clerk in county where event occurred has earlier records.

KENTUCKY
Office of Vital Statistics Department of Health Statistics
275 E. Main St.
Frankfort, KY 40621
Phone: 502-564-4212
BIRTH and DEATH: State has records since January 1911 and some earlier records for Louisville, Newport, Lexington and Covington.

LOUISIANA
Division of Vital Records Office of Health Services and Environmental Quality
P.O. Box 60630
New Orleans, LA 70160
Phone: 504-568-5175
BIRTH and DEATH: State has most records since July 1914. State has birth records from 1790 and death records from 1803 for city of New Orleans.

MAINE
Office of Vital Records
Human Services Building
State House, Station 11
Augusta, ME 04333
Phone: 207-289-3181
BIRTH and DEATH: State has records since 1892. For earlier records, contact municipality where event occurred.

MARYLAND
Division of Vital Records
State Department of Health
State Office Building P.O. Box 13146
201 W. Preston St.
Baltimore, MD 21203
Phone: 301-225-5988
BIRTH and DEATH: State has most records since 1898 and some Baltimore records from 1875.

MASSACHUSETTS
Registry of Vital Statistics
150 Tremont St., Room B-3
Boston, MA 02111
Phone: 617- 727-0110
BIRTH and DEATH: State has records since 1896. For earlier records, contact State Archives, State House, Boston.

MICHIGAN
Office of State Registrar
Center for Health Statistics
Michigan Department of Public Health
3500 N. Logan St.
Lansing, MI 48909
Phone: 517-335-8655
BIRTH and DEATH: State has records since 1867. County Clerk in county where event occurred also has record. Detroit City Health Department has birth records since 1893 and death records since 1897.

MINNESOTA
Minnesota Department of Health
Section of Vital Statistics
717 Delaware St. S.E.
Minneapolis, MN 55440
Phone: 612-623-5121
BIRTH and DEATH: State has records since January 1908. For earlier records, contact Court Administrator in the county where event occurred. If the birth or death occurred in St. Paul, contact St. Paul City Health Department.

MISSISSIPPI
Vital Records State Board of Health
P.O. Box 1700
Jackson MS 39215

Phone: 601-354-6606
BIRTH and DEATH: State office has records since 1912.

MISSOURI
State Department of Health
Bureau of Vital Records
P.O. Box 570
Jefferson City, MO 65102
Phone: 314-751-6376
BIRTH and DEATH: State has records since January 1910. For St. Louis, St. Louis County or Kansas City records before 1910, write city or county health department.

MONTANA
Bureau of Records & Statistics
State Department of Health
Helena, MT 59620
Phone: 406-444-2614
BIRTH and DEATH: State has records since late 1907.

NEBRASKA
Bureau of Vital Statistics
State Department of Health
301 Centennial Mall South P.O. Box 95007
Lincoln, NE 68509
Phone: 402-471-2871
BIRTH and DEATH: State has records since late 1904 and can provide information about earlier birth records.

NEVADA
Division of Health Vital Statistics
Capitol Complex
Carson City, NV 89710
Phone: 702-885-4480
BIRTH and DEATH: State has records since July 1911. For earlier records, contact County Recorder in county where event occurred.

NEW HAMPSHIRE
Bureau of Vital Records
Human Services Building
6 Hazen Drive
Concord, NH 03301
Phone: 603-271-4654
BIRTH and DEATH: State has some records since 1640.

NEW JERSEY
State Department of Health
Bureau of Vital Statistics CN 360
Trenton, NJ 08625
Phone: 609-292-4087
BIRTH, DEATH and MARRIAGE: State has records since May 1878. For records from May 1848 to May 1878, contact Archives and History Bureau, State Library Division, State Department of Education, Trenton, N.J. 08625.

NEW MEXICO
Vital Statistics Bureau
New Mexico Health Services Division
P.O. Box 968
Santa Fe, NM 87504
(505) 827-2338 BIRTH and DEATH: State has records since 1920.

NEW YORK (EXCEPT NEW YORK CITY)
Bureau of Vital Records State
Department of Health
Empire State Plaza Tower Building
Albany, NY 12237
Phone: 518-474-3075
BIRTH and DEATH: State has records since 1880. For records before 1914 in Albany, Buffalo and Yonkers or before 1880 in any other city, check Registrar of Vital Statistics in city where event occurred.

NEW YORK CITY (ALL BOROUGHS)
Bureau of Vital Records
Department of Health of New York City
125 Worth St.
New York, NY 10013
Phone: 212-619-4530
BIRTH and DEATH: City has birth records since 1898 and death records since 1920. For earlier records, check Archives Division, Department of Records and Information Services, 31 Chambers St., New York, NY 10007.

NORTH CAROLINA
Department of Human Resources
Division of Health Services Vital Records Branch
P.O. Box 2091
Raleigh, NC 27602
Phone: 919-733-3526
BIRTH and DEATH: State office has birth records since October 1913 and death records since January 1930. Death records from 1913 to 1929 are available from Archives and Records Section, State Records Center, 215 North Blount St., Raleigh, NC 27602.

NORTH DAKOTA
Division of Vital Records
State Department of Health
Office of Statistical Services
Bismarck, ND 58505
Phone: 701-224-2360
BIRTH and DEATH: State has some records since July 1983, although years from 1894 to 1920 are incomplete.

OHIO
Division of Vital Statistics Ohio
Department of Health
G-20 Ohio Department Building
65 S. Front St.
Columbus, OH 43266
(614) 466-2531
BIRTH and DEATH: State has records since December 1908. For earlier records, check Probate Court in county where event occurred.

OKLAHOMA
Vital Records Section
State Department of Health
N.E. 10th St. and Stonewall
P.O. Box 53551
Oklahoma City, OK 73152
Phone: 405-271-4040
BIRTH and DEATH: State has records since 1908.

OREGON
Oregon State Health Division
Vital Statistics Section
P.O. Box 116
Portland, OR 97207
Phone: 503-299-5710
BIRTH and DEATH: State has records since July 1903. Some earlier records for city of Portland since 1880 available from Oregon State Archives, 1005 Broadway N.E., Salem OR 97310

PENNSYLVANIA
Division of Vital Records
State Department of Health Central Building
101 S. Mercer St. P.O. Box 1528
New Castle, PA 16103
Phone: 724-656-3100
BIRTH and DEATH: State has records since 1906. For earlier records, contact Registrar of Wills, Orphans Court, in county seat where event occurred. For birth and death records in Pittsburgh from 1870 to 1905, contact Office of Biostatistics, Pittsburgh Health Department, City-County Building, Pittsburgh, PA 15219. For birth and death records in Philadelphia from 1860 to 1915, contact Vital Statistics, Philadelphia Department of Public Health, City Hall Annex, Philadelphia, PA 19107.

PUERTO RICO
Division of Demographic Registry and Vital Statistics
Department of Health
San Juan, PR 00909
Phone: 809-728-4300
BIRTH and DEATH: Central office has records since July 22, 1931. For earlier records, contact local Registrar in town where event occurred.

RHODE ISLAND
Division of Vital Statistics
State Department of Health
Cannon Building, Room 101
75 Davis
St. Providence, RI 02908
Phone: 401-277-2811
BIRTH and DEATH: State has records since 1853. Fore earlier records, contact Town Clerk in town where event occurred.

SOUTH CAROLINA
Office of Vital Records and Public Health Statistics
State Department of Health
2600 Bull St.
Columbia, SC 29201
Phone: 803-734-4830
BIRTH and DEATH: State office has records since January 1915. The City of Charleston has birth records from 1877 and death records from 1821 on file at Charleston County Health Department.

SOUTH DAKOTA
State Department of Health
Center for Health Policy and Statistics
523 E. Capitol
Pierre, SD 57501
Phone: 605-773-3355
BIRTH and DEATH: State has records since 1905.

TENNESSEE
Tennessee Vital Records Department of Health
Cordell Hull Building
Nashville, TN 37219
Phone: 615-741-1763
BIRTH and DEATH: State has birth records for entire state since 1914; Nashville since 1881; Knoxville since 1881 and Chattanooga since 1882. Death records are available for entire state since 1914; Chattanooga since 1872; Knoxville since 1887; and Nashville since 1874. For Memphis records, check Memphis-Shelby County Health Department, Division of Vital Records, Memphis, TN 38105.

TEXAS
Bureau of Vital Statistics
Texas Department of Health
1100 West 49th St.
Austin, TX 78756
Phone: 512-458-7380
BIRTH and DEATH: State has records since 1903.

UTAH
Bureau of Vital Records
Utah Department of Health
288 North 1460 West
P.O. Box 16700
Salt Lake City, UT 84116
Phone: 801-538-6105
BIRTH and DEATH: State has records since 1905. If birth or death occurred from 1890 to 1904 in Salt Lake City or Ogden, contact City Board of Health. For other records, contact County Clerk in county where birth or death occurred.

VERMONT
Vermont Department of Health
Vital Records Section
Box 70 60 Main St.
Burlington, VT 05402
Phone: 802-863-7275
BIRTH, DEATH and MARRIAGE: State has records since 1955. For earlier records, contact Division of Public Records, 6 Baldwin St., Montpelier, Vt. 05602.

VIRGINIA
Division of Vital Records
State Department of Health
James Madison Building
P.O. Box 1000
Richmond, VA 23208
Phone: 804-786-6228
BIRTH and DEATH: State has records from January 1853 to December 1896 and since June 14, 1912. For records between those dates, contact Health Department in the city where the birth or death occurred.

WASHINGTON
Vital Records
P.O. Box 9790, ET-11
Olympia, WA 98504
Phone: 206-753-5396
BIRTH and DEATH: State has records since July 1907. For earlier records, contact the County Auditor in county where birth or death occurred.

WEST VIRGINIA
Division of Vital Statistics State Department of Health State Office Bldg., No. 3 Charleston, WV 25305 Phone: 304-348-2931 BIRTH and DEATH: State has records since January 1917. For earlier records, contact Clerk of County Court in the county where the birth or death occurred.

WISCONSIN
Bureau of Health Statistics
Wisconsin Division of Health
P.O. Box 309
Madison, WI 53701
Phone: 608-266-1371
BIRTH and DEATH: State has records from October 1907, and some incomplete records back to 1857.

WYOMING
Vital Records Services
Division of Health and Medical Services
Hathaway Building
Cheyenne, WY 82002
Phone: 307-777-7591
BIRTH and DEATH: State has records from July 1909.

MAJOR U.S. GENEALOGICAL SOCIETIES

Federation of Genealogical Societies (FGS)
is a non-profit organization comprised of hundreds of genealogical and historical societies, family associations, and libraries. Its directory contains a comprehensive listing of genealogical and historical societies in the United States.
P.O. Box 200940
Austin, TX 78720-0940
Phone: 888-47-1500
Web:

National Genealogical Society Library (NGS) -
contains about 30,000 books of family history and local history, Members Ancestral Charts, Bible Records and Family History Files.
4527 17th St., N.,
Arlington, VA 22207-2399
Phone: 703-25-0050
Phone: 800-473-0060
Web:

National Society of the Daughters of the American Revolution - contains local history in America, embracing state, county, town and church materials, genealogies, biographies and vital records. These histories provide the link in connecting ancestors of the Revolutionary period with today's descendants.

1776 D. Street
Washington D.C. 20006-5303
Phone: 202-628-1776
Web: <www.dar.org/library/library.html>

New England Historic Genealogical Society -
contains resources on New England families and extensive materials from other regions of the USA, as well as Canada, Great Britain, and Europe.
101 Newbury Street
Boston, MA 02116
Phone: 617- 536-5740
Web:

MAJOR WORLD WIDE WEBSITES THAT CONTAIN INSTRUCTIONS OR RECORDS ONLINE

Ancestors - KBYU-TV, in association with the Public Broadcasting System's television series titled Ancestors presents online instruction, links and resources for family history research.
Web: <www2.kbyu.org/ancestors/>

Ancestry.com - Provides access to a limited number of free databases. Membership required to access numerous commercial databases. Ancestry.com also operates FamilyHistory.com and MyFamily.com.
Web:

Common Threads - contains a searchable surname database of ancestral entries made by genealogist using the Internet.
Web: <www.gensource.com/common/index.htm>

Cyndi's List of Genealogical Sites on the Internet -
Contains multiple search indexes that list tens of thousands of genealogy links to information and records.
Web:

Everton's Genealogical Helper - online magazine, searchable databases, resources, references.
Web: <www.everton.com>

FamilySearch Internet Genealogy Service - provides access to free online databases that contain hundreds of millions of names and extensive genealogical resources gathered by The Church of Jesus Christ of Latter-day Saints.
Web: <http://www.familysearch.org/>

FamilyTreeMaker - provides access to over 1 billion names.
Web:

Genealogy.com - this portal provides databases, forums, tutorials and links to commercial services.
Web: <http://www.genealogy.com/>

GenWeb Project Web Sites - The GenWeb Project Web Sites are maintained by volunteers working together to provide access to websites for genealogical research.
The US GenWeb Project
Web:
The Canada GenWeb Project
Web: <www.rootsweb.com/~canwgw/>
The World GenWeb Project

Web: <http://worldgenweb.org/>

Rootsweb - The Internet's oldest and largest free genealogical site.
Web:

Society Hill Directory - Lists over 5000 Genealogical societies in the United States, Canada and Australia.
Web: <www.daddezio.com/society/>

SurnameWeb - provides search engines to almost 2 billion records and 100,000 genealogy links.
Web:

USGenExchange - is a non- commercial genealogical data exchange and surname registry that allows visitors and researchers to exchange data with one another.
Web: <www.genexchange.com/us.cfm/>

Vital Records Information - contains links to U.S. and international vital records offfices, adoption resources, surname searches and investigative services.
Web: <www.vitalrec.com/links.html>

When you have found an archive or genealogical society near you, return to Step 3e on page 22.

GLOSSARY

Ancestors - People from whom one is descended, especially a relative more distant than a grandparent; forefathers.

Background Information - Records that deal with geographical, historical, or cultural information. They include local histories, maps, gazetteers, language dictionaries, and guidebooks. These records can help you learn about the area where your ancestors lived and the events that may have affected their lives.

Biographical Events - Events that happened in the life of a person, including birth, christening, marriage and death.

Cataloger - One who classifies records and publications according to a categorical system.

Consistency - 1. Agreement or logical coherence among things or parts. 2. Reliability or uniformity of successive results or events.

Custodian - One that has charge of something; a caretaker.

E-mail - Electronic mail allows computer users send and receive text messages, graphics, and sometimes sounds and animated images to other users.

Evidence - 1. A thing or things helpful in forming a conclusion or judgment. 2. Something indicative; an outward sign.

Eyewitness - An individual present at an event, such as a marriage or the signing of a document, who can vouch that the event took place.

Family Group Record - A standard form for recording genealogical information about one family — a husband, a wife and their children. It usually includes the dates and places of birth, marriage and death.

Family History Center - A local branch of The Church of Jesus Christ of Latter-day Saints' Family History Library in Salt Lake City, Utah. These centers are free and open to the public. Visitors may use family history computer programs and databases developed by the Church, search the Family History Center's book and microfilm collection, or for a small fee order microfilms from the Family History Library collection. There are more than 3,500 Family History Centers located in 64 countries throughout the world.

Family History Library - This library in Salt Lake City, Utah is operated by The Church of Jesus Christ of Latter-day Saints and houses the largest collection of genealogical records in the world. It is free and open to the public. It holds over 2 million rolls of microfilmed records, 400,000 microfiche, and 300,000 books. It also houses an extensive collection of written manuscripts including family histories, local histories, indexes, periodicals, and aids to help in genealogical research.

Family History Library Catalog - This is a listing of the records, books, microfilm, and microfiche available at the Family History Library. The catalog is available on computer, microfiche, and the www.familysearch.org website

FamilySearch Internet Genealogy Service (www.familysearch.org) - A World Wide Web service sponsored by The Church of Jesus Christ of Latter-day Saints to help people find and share family history information. It allows access to the Family History Library Catalog, International Genealogical Index, and Ancestral File. It also allows users to preserve their genealogy, collaborate with others and link to other genealogical websites.

Genealogy - 1. The science or study of family descent. 2. A chart or recorded history of the descent of a person or family from an ancestor or ancestors. 3. Descent from an ancestor; pedigree; lineage.

Generation - 1. All of the offspring that are at the same stage of descent from a common ancestor. 2. The average interval of time between the birth of parents and the birth of their offspring. 3. A group of individuals born and living about the same time that share common cultural or social characteristics and attitudes.

Hearsay Witness - Someone who has indirect knowledge of an event.

Indirectness - Not proceeding straight to the point or object.

Internet - A vast electronic communications network that connects computer networks across the world.

Jurisdiction - 1. Authority or control. 2. The extent of authority or control. 3. The territorial range of authority or control.

Legacy - A gift by will, given by or received from an ancestor or predecessor or from the past.

Meta Search - A computer program that looks through a number of search engines on the World Wide Web and returns results based on a keyword or phrase.

Microfiche - A card or sheet of microfilm capable of accommodating and preserving a considerable number of pages, as of printed text, in reduced form.

Microfilm - 1. A film on which printed materials are photographed at greatly reduced size for ease of storage. 2. A reproduction on microfilm.

Paleography - The study of ancient forms of writing.

Pedigree Chart - A standard genealogical form for recording an individual's ancestry. It usually includes a person's parents, grandparents, great-grandparents, and so on, but does not include brothers, sisters, aunts, uncles, and other relatives.

Periodical - A publication issued at regular intervals.

Record Repository - A place where records are put for safekeeping. Repositories may include libraries, archives, or government and church offices.

Relevant - Having a bearing on or connection with the matter at hand.

Reliable Sources - People, places or objects that can be depended upon for accuracy.

Research Log - A written document that lists each record searched and the information found.

Research Objective - A goal to achieve through genealogical research. For example, an objective may be to find an unknown date, name or place, or to verify information.

Search Engine - A program which acts like a library card catalog for the Internet. It locates information based on a keyword or phrase specified by the user.

Source Information - Important details about a person, place, or object from which you can obtain information.

Source Notes - A form used to record information you obtain from people, objects and records.

Surname - Family name or last name; name added to a "given" name, in many cases inherited and held in common by members of a family.

Surname Organization - Individuals with the same last name and or have a common interest in a specific last name. The organization provides a forum for researchers to share methodology and ideas, as well as to exchange family genealogy.

Unverified - Lacking proof or substantiation.

Vital Events - Important events in a person's life, including birth, christening, marriage, and death.

QUICK GUIDE TO FAMILY HISTORY SOURCES

Research Principles and Processes

Carmack, Sharon DeBartolo, *Organizing Your Family History Search: Efficient & Effective Ways to Gather and Protect Your Genealogical Research* (Cincinnati, Ohio: Betterway Books, 1999)

Chamberlin, David C., The *Conceptual Approach To Genealogy* (Bountiful, UT: Heritage Quest, 1998)

Croom, Emily Anne, *The Genealogist's Companion & Sourcebook* (Cincinnati, Ohio: Betterway Books, 1999)

Croom, Emily Anne, *Unpuzzling Your Past: A Basic Guide to Genealogy* (Cincinnati, Ohio: Betterway Books, 1995)

Hartley, William G., *The Everything Family Tree Book: Finding, Charting, and Preserving Your Family History* (Holbrook, Masschussetts: Adams Media Corp., 1998)

Hinckley, Kathleen W., *Locating Lost Family Members & Friends : Modern Genealogical Research Techniques for Locating the People of Your Past and Present* (Cincinnati, Ohio: Betterway Books, 1999)

Whitaker, Beverly Delong, *Beyond Pedigrees : Organizing and Enhancing Your Work* (Orem, Utah: Ancestry, Inc., 1993)

Willard, Jim and Terry, with Jane Wilson, *Ancestors* (New York: Houghton Mifflin Co., 1997)

Wolfman, Ira, *Do People Grow on Family Trees? Genealogy for Kids and Other Beginners* (New York: Workman Publishing Company, Inc. 1991)

Descriptions of Record Types

Luebking, Sandra H. (Editor), Szucs, Loretto D., *The Source: A Guidebook of American Genealogy*, Revised edition (Orem, Utah: Ancestry, Inc., 1997)

Westin, Jeane Eddy, *Finding Your Roots: How to Trace Your Ancestors at Home and Abroad* (New York: Jeremy P. Tarcher/Putnam, 1998)

Places Where Records Are Stored

Bentley, Elizabeth Petty, *The Genealogist's Address Book*, 4th edition (Baltimore, Maryland: Genealogical Publishing Co., 1998)

Dollarhide, William and Bremer, Ronald A., *America's Best Genealogy Resource Centers* (Bountiful, UT: Heritage Quest, 1998)

Smith, Juliana Szucs, compiler, *The Ancestry Family Historian's Address Book: A Comprehensive List of Addresses of Local, State, & Federal Agencies & Institutions* (Orem, Utah: Ancestry, Inc., 1998)

How To Use Computers and the Internet

Arends, Marthe, *Genealogy Software Guide*, 1st edition (Baltimore, Maryland: Genealogical Publishing Co., 1998)

Bonner, Laurie and Steve, *Searching for Cyber-Roots* (Orem, Utah: Ancestry, Inc., 1997)

Helm, Matthew L. and Helm, April Leigh, *Genealogy Online for Dummies*, 2nd edition (Foster City, California: IDG Books Worldwide, 1999)

Howells, Cyndi, *Netting Your Ancestors: Genealogical Research on the Internet* (Baltimore, Maryland: Genealogical Publishing Co., 1997)

Maran, Ruth, *Teach Yourself Computers & the Internet Visually*, 2nd edition (Foster City, California: IDG Books Worldwide, 1997)

Ways to Preserve Information

Crichton, Jennifer, *Family Reunion* (New York: Workman Publishing Company, 1998)

Epstein, Ellen and Lewit, Jand, *Record and Remember: Tracing Your Roots Through Oral History* (Lanham, Maryland: Scarborogh House, 1994)

Hartley, William G., *The Everything Family Tree Book: Finding, Charting, and Preserving Your Family History* (Holbrook, Masschussetts: Adams Media Corp., 1998)

Hatcher, Patricia Law, *Producing a Quality Family History* (Orem, Utah: Ancestry, Inc., 1997)

Slan, Joanna Campbell, *Scrapbook Storytelling: Save Family Stories and Memories With Photos, Journaling and Your Own Creativity* (Writers Digest Books, 1999)

How To Cite and Evaluate Evidence

Mills, Elizabeth Shown, *Evidence!: Citation & Analysis for the Family Historian* (Baltimore, Maryland: Genealogical Publishing Co., 1997)

Stevenson, Noel C., *Genealogical Evidence - A Guide to the Standard of Proof Relating to Pedigrees, Ancestry, Heirship and Family History* (Laguna Hills, California: Aegean Park Press, 1979)

Family Group Record

Page_____ of_____

Write names as:
James Henry WRIGHT

Write dates as:
30 Mar 1974

Write places as:
Tryon, Polk, North Carolina, USA
or St. Andrew, Rugby, Warwick, England

Husband Given name(s)		Last name	☐ See "Other Marriages"
Born (day month year)	Place		
Died	Place		
Buried	Place		
Married	Place		
Husband's father Given name(s)		Last name	
Husband's mother Given name(s)		Last name	
Wife Given name(s)		Last name	☐ See "Other Marriages"
Born (day month year)	Place		
Died	Place		
Buried	Place		
Married	Place		
Wife's father Given name(s)		Last name	
Wife's mother Given name(s)		Last name	

Children List each child (whether living or dead) in order of birth.

1

Female ☐	Given name(s)		Last name	☐ See "Other Marriages"
	Born (day month year)	Place		
	Died	Place		
	Buried	Place		
Male ☐	Spouse Given name(s)		Last name	
	Married	Place		

2

Female ☐	Given name(s)		Last name	☐ See "Other Marriages"
	Born (day month year)	Place		
	Died	Place		
	Buried	Place		
Male ☐	Spouse Given name(s)		Last name	
	Married	Place		

3

Female ☐	Given name(s)		Last name	☐ See "Other Marriages"
	Born (day month year)	Place		
	Died	Place		
	Buried	Place		
Male ☐	Spouse Given name(s)		Last name	
	Married	Place		

Other Marriages

Children List each child (whether living or dead) in order of birth.

4	Given name(s)		Last name	☐ See "Other Marriages"
Female ☐	Born (day month year)	Place		
	Died	Place		
	Buried	Place		
Male ☐	Spouse Given name(s)		Last name	
	Married	Place		

5	Given name(s)		Last name	☐ See "Other Marriages"
Female ☐	Born (day month year)	Place		
	Died	Place		
	Buried	Place		
Male ☐	Spouse Given name(s)		Last name	
	Married	Place		

6	Given name(s)		Last name	☐ See "Other Marriages"
Female ☐	Born (day month year)	Place		
	Died	Place		
	Buried	Place		
Male ☐	Spouse Given name(s)		Last name	
	Married	Place		

7	Given name(s)		Last name	☐ See "Other Marriages"
Female ☐	Born (day month year)	Place		
	Died	Place		
	Buried	Place		
Male ☐	Spouse Given name(s)		Last name	
	Married	Place		

8	Given name(s)		Last name	☐ See "Other Marriages"
Female ☐	Born (day month year)	Place		
	Died	Place		
	Buried	Place		
Male ☐	Spouse Given name(s)		Last name	
	Married	Place		

Other Marriages

Sources

ANCESTORS

Research Questions

Page____

Ancestor's name: _____
First   Middle   Last (Maiden)

☐ Male
☐ Female

This person is on pedigree chart number ____, line number ____, and/or is child number ____ on the family group record of (Husband's name):

_____

Born: _____ Married: _____ Died: _____

I need information about:	Questions to answer about information needed	Possible information sources

Events:
☐ Adoption
☐ Birth
☐ Burial
☐ Court (transaction)
☐ Cremation
☐ Death
☐ Divorce
☐ Emigration
☐ Illness
☐ Immigration
☐ Imprisonment
☐ Land (ownership)
☐ Marriage
☐ Migration
☐ Military (service)
☐ Naturalization
☐ Occupation
☐ Orphaned
☐ Probate (will)
☐ Religious (activity)
☐ Residence
☐ School
☐ Taxation

Relationships:
☐ Brother
☐ Child/ Children
☐ Father
☐ Grandparents
☐ Half-(relative)
☐ Mother
☐ Parents
☐ Siblings
☐ Sister
☐ Spouse
☐ Step-(relative)

Descriptions:
☐ Age
☐ Biography
☐ Physical appearance

Places:
☐ History
☐ Geography
☐ Culture
☐ Language
☐ Facts

Other:
_____

© KBYU 2000

Research Questions

A N C E S T O R S

Ancestor's
name: _____

First   Middle   Last (Maiden)

☐ Male
☐ Female

Born: _____ Married: _____ Died: _____

This person is on pedigree chart number ____,
line number ____ , <u>and/or</u> is child number ____
on the family group record of (Husband's name):

_____

I need information about:	Questions to answer about information needed	Possible information sources
Events: ☐ Adoption ☐ Birth ☐ Burial ☐ Court (transaction) ☐ Cremation ☐ Death ☐ Divorce ☐ Emigration ☐ Illness ☐ Immigration ☐ Imprisonment ☐ Land (ownership) ☐ Marriage ☐ Migration ☐ Military (service) ☐ Naturalization ☐ Occupation ☐ Orphaned ☐ Probate (will) ☐ Religious (activity) ☐ Residence ☐ School ☐ Taxation **Relationships:** ☐ Brother ☐ Child/ Children ☐ Father ☐ Grandparents ☐ Half-(relative) ☐ Mother ☐ Parents ☐ Siblings ☐ Sister ☐ Spouse ☐ Step-(relative) **Descriptions:** ☐ Age ☐ Biography ☐ Physical appearance **Places:** ☐ History ☐ Geography ☐ Culture ☐ Language ☐ Facts **Other:**		

Research Log

Page____

Ancestor's name: _____

First   Middle   Last (Maiden)

Born: Married: Died:

☐ Male
☐ Female

This person is on pedigree chart number ____, line number ____ , and/or is child number ____ on the family group record of (Husband's name):
_____

Research objective: Question about an event, relationship, place, or subject	Name and Location of source. Include name and address of the source person, object or record repository. When it applies, include title, author, publisher of book, document, writing, electronic database, web site, etc.	Search Date	Notes about source. May include a: reason for its selection, description of its condition, summary and analysis of information found, etc.	File number you assigned to notes/copy made of information from source

Research Log

Page____

Ancestor's name: _____

First　　　　Middle　　　　Last (Maiden)

Born: _____　Married: _____　Died: _____

☐ Male
☐ Female

This person is on pedigree chart number ____, line number ____ , and/or is child number ____ on the family group record of (Husband's name):

_____

Research objective: Question about an event, relationship, place, or subject	Name and Location of source. Include name and address of the source person, object or record repository. When it applies, include title, author, publisher of book, document, writing, electronic database, web site, etc.	Search Date	Notes about source. May include a: reason for its selection, description of its condition, summary and analysis of information found, etc.	File number you assigned to notes/copy made of information from source

Source Notes

Ancestor's name: _____

☐ Male
☐ Female

First　　　　Middle　　　　Last (Maiden)

Born: 　　　Married: 　　　Died:

This person is on pedigree chart number ____, line number ____ , and/or is child number ____ on the family group record of (Husband's name)

File Number:

This source contains information about:

☐ **Person**　　☐ **Object**　　☐ **Record**

Events:
- ☐ Adoption
- ☐ Birth
- ☐ Burial
- ☐ Citizenship
- ☐ Court (transaction)
- ☐ Cremation
- ☐ Death
- ☐ Divorce
- ☐ Emigration
- ☐ Illness
- ☐ Immigration
- ☐ Imprisonment
- ☐ Land (ownership)
- ☐ Marriage
- ☐ Migration
- ☐ Military (service)
- ☐ Naturalization
- ☐ Occupation
- ☐ Orphaned
- ☐ Probate (will)
- ☐ Religious (activity)
- ☐ Residence
- ☐ School
- ☐ Taxation

Relationships:
- ☐ Brother
- ☐ Child/ Children
- ☐ Father
- ☐ Grandparents
- ☐ Half-(relative)
- ☐ Mother
- ☐ Parents
- ☐ Siblings
- ☐ Sister
- ☐ Spouse
- ☐ Step-(relative)

Descriptions:
- ☐ Age
- ☐ Biography
- ☐ Physical appearance

Places:
- ☐ History
- ☐ Geography
- ☐ Culture
- ☐ Language
- ☐ Facts

Name of Source *Person or Object*

Location or Address of *Person or Object*

City　　　　State　　　　Zip Code

Country

Phone number

Title of Source *Record*

Author/Editor/Compiler:

Publisher

Place of Publication　　　　Date

Volume #　　Page #　　Call # / Microfilm/fiche #

Location or Address of Source Record

Website address

Notes about source. May include: a reason for selection, a description of condition, summary of results, analysis of information found, etc.

Source Notes

Date: _____

Ancestor's name: _____

First　　　Middle　　　Last (Maiden)

Born:　　　Married:　　　Died:

☐ Male
☐ Female

This person is on pedigree chart number _____, line number _____ , and/or is child number _____ on the family group record of (Husband's name):

_____

Pedigree Chart

No. 1 on this chart is the same as
No. _____ on pedigree chart no. _____

Write names as: James Henry WRIGHT
Write dates as: 30 Mar 1974
Write places as: Tryon, Polk, North Carolina, USA
or St. Andrew, Rugby, Warwick, England

2

FATHER (of no. 1)
Born
Place

Married
Place

Died
Place

1

_____
(Name)
Born
Place

Married
Place

Died
Place

_____
SPOUSE (of no. 1)

3

MOTHER (of no. 1)
Born
Place

Died
Place

4

FATHER (of no. 2)
Born
Place

Married
Place

Died
Place

5

MOTHER (of no. 2)
Born
Place

Died
Place

6

FATHER (of no. 3)
Born
Place

Married
Place

Died
Place

7

MOTHER (of no. 3)
Born
Place

Died
Place

8

FATHER (of no. 4)
Born
Place
Married
Place
Died
Place

Cont. on
chart no.
_____

9

MOTHER (of no. 4)
Born
Place
Died
Place

Cont. on
chart no.
_____

10

FATHER (of no. 5)
Born
Place
Married
Place
Died
Place

Cont. on
chart no.
_____

11

MOTHER (of no. 5)
Born
Place
Died
Place

Cont. on
chart no.
_____

12

FATHER (of no. 6)
Born
Place
Married
Place
Died
Place

Cont. on
chart no.
_____

13

MOTHER (of no. 6)
Born
Place
Died
Place

Cont. on
chart no.
_____

14

FATHER (of no. 7)
Born
Place
Married
Place
Died
Place

Cont. on
chart no.
_____

15

MOTHER (of no. 7)
Born
Place
Died
Place

Cont. on
chart no.
_____

ABOUT THE AUTHOR

Jim Tyrrell is an instructional designer and family historian. He has been a consultant for the PBS television series *Ancestors* and author of *Ancestors - Companion Teacher's Guide*.

He has developed courses, organized seminars and conferences, designed a variety of instructional materials, and taught thousands of trainers in the principles and processes of helping others with their family history research.

He is married to the former Rita Leavitt and they have seven children.